FOUNDED 1848
INCORPORATED
WAYLAND
EAST SUDBURY 1780.
FOUNDED 1635.
1835

BOOKS BY

Stanley Edgar Hyman

POETRY AND CRITICISM 1961

Four Revolutions in Literary Taste

THE CRITICAL PERFORMANCE 1956

An Anthology of American and British Literary Criticism of Our Century

THE ARMED VISION 1948

A Study in the Methods of Modern Literary Criticism

POETRY
AND
CRITICISM

POETRY AND CRITICISM

FOUR REVOLUTIONS IN LITERARY TASTE

Stanley Edgar Hyman

NEW YORK

ATHENEUM

1961

Quotations from T. S. Eliot's "Sweeney Among the Nightingales" are from COLLECTED POEMS 1909–1935, *copyright, 1936, by Harcourt, Brace and Company, Inc. and used with their permission; quotations from T. S. Eliot's "Tradition and the Individual Talent" are from* SELECTED ESSAYS OF T. S. ELIOT, *copyright, 1932, 1936, by Harcourt, Brace and Company, Inc., and used with their permission.*

Quotations from T. S. Eliot's "The Music of Poetry" and his essay on Milton are from ON POETRY AND POETS, *copyright 1943, © 1957 by T. S. Eliot; used by permission of the publisher, Farrar, Straus and Cudahy, Inc.*

Quotations from David Grene's translation of OEDIPUS THE KING, *and Rex Warner's translation of* MEDEA *are used with the permission of the publisher, The University of Chicago Press.*

Quotations from Ingram Bywater's translation of Aristotle's POETICS *are used with the permission of the publisher, Oxford University Press, Inc.*

Quotations from W. Rhys Roberts' translation of LONGINUS ON THE SUBLIME *are used with the permission of the publisher, Cambridge University Press.*

Library of Congress catalog card number 61-6741
Published simultaneously in Canada by
Longmans, Green & Company
Manufactured in the United States of America by
Kingsport Press, Inc., Kingsport, Tennessee
Designed by Harry Ford
First Edition

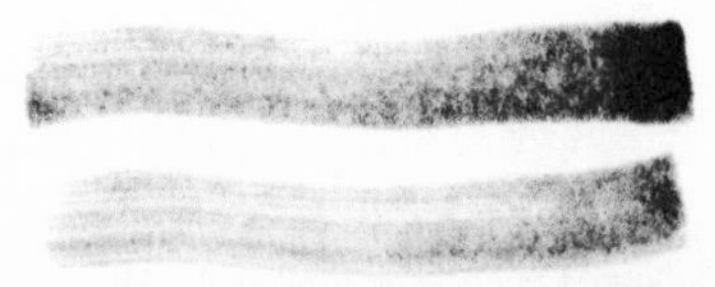

To my parents

Acknowledgments

THESE FOUR ESSAYS were delivered, in slightly shorter form, as a series of public lectures sponsored by the Department of English of Wayne State University in 1960. I am grateful to Herbert M. Schueller and the department for the opportunity, and to my audience at Wayne State for a good deal of stimulating and useful discussion. The writing of the book was enormously facilitated by a fellowship from the American Council of Learned Societies, and I must particularly acknowledge the kindness of Frederick H. Burkhardt and Miss Charlotte Bowman of the Council. Portions of the book have appeared in *The American Scholar*, *The Centennial Review*, and *The Hudson Review*, whose permission to reprint them is gratefully acknowledged.

My students and colleagues at Bennington College, who have educated me over the years, can fairly be considered co-authors of this work, as can students and colleagues at Columbia University in 1959. Miss Mary S. Hopkins and the staff of the Bennington College Library have been endlessly helpful, as have Simon Michael Bessie, Harry Ford, and the staff of Atheneum Publishers. Miss Isabel Sherwood typed the manuscript and read my handwriting with a skill dangerously close to necromancy. The friends who read the manuscript, and the critics I quote or have learned from too deeply for quotation, are most gratefully acknowledged. My wife, Shirley Jackson, has again helped beyond the possibilities of acknowledgment.

S. E. H.

North Bennington, Vermont, January, 1961

Contents

POETRY
AND
CRITICISM

Introduction

If we seek to understand literary criticism, not in isolation, but in relation to the poetry that is its subject-matter and perhaps its justification, we would do well to discard the idea that great critics call great poets into being. The true relation seems rather to be the reverse; revolutions in criticism follow after revolutions in poetry, sometimes long after, codifying and consolidating them. When a critic makes a general statement about all poetry, he tends to have some particular poetry in mind, which he takes to be the ideal. We can best see this by reducing the multiplicity of literature in any given period to four representative specimens. A is the original poem, which we will call the *standard*. B is the criticism that erects the A poem's formal organization into general principles, the *poetics*. C is the new or deviant work that cannot be accommodated to the critical principles of B, and we will call it the *challenge*. D is the new critical generalization that arises out of and justifies C, and it might be called the *sanction*.

In literary history, this movement is a continuing dialectic, and the challenge and sanction of one series become the standard and poetics of the next, and provoke a new C and D into being. For our purposes in these lectures, four lengths of this endless ribbon will be artificially cut off to show the A, B, C and D of Ancient Greek literature, English Neo-Classicism, English Romanticism, and the modern revolution. It should be obvious that the critic producing the poetics or sanction may be, and often is, himself the author of the standard or challenge poem. He may on the other hand not even know the poem, may dislike it, or may come so long after it in time that it does not particularly interest him. In either case, the critic's statements are best understood in terms of that poem, and by making overt the ties of literary criticism to specific works of imaginative literature, we can hope to gain new insights into the critical performance, and perhaps into the creative performance too.

I

Ancient Greek Literature

For the Greeks, our STANDARD OF A work is Sophocles' *Oedipus the King*. It was written and produced in Athens sometime around 430 B.C., and the group of plays that included it did not win a prize in the civic competition. Our play tells the story of Oedipus, as ruler of Thebes, seeking to discover the unknown murderer of Laius, the former king, and end the pestilence caused the city by that unexpiated crime. In the course of the play's action he discovers that he is both the son and murderer of Laius, as well as the son and husband of Jocasta, and that he has killed his father and married his mother as the oracles predicted. Jocasta hangs herself, and Oedipus puts out his eyes and sentences himself to banishment. My quotations are from David Grene's translation.

In *The Idea of a Theater*, Francis Fergusson takes *Oedipus the King* as an ideal example of the tragic movement, which he calls from Purpose through Passion to Perception. Finding Laius's slayer is the purpose, the suffering involved in the discoveries is the passion, and the recognition at the end the perception. Fergusson writes: "This movement, or *tragic rhythm of action*, constitutes the shape of the play as a whole; it is also the shape of each episode, each discussion between principals with the chorus following." We may see the action in related terms primarily as a quest, like that of the hero in mythology, going down into the dark underworld or the dragon's lair. At each stage Oedipus is warned and even implored not to pursue his quest further. Teiresias, the old blind seer first consulted, repeatedly asks to be released to go home, refuses to cooperate in the inquiry, and finally, provoked, threatens:

> This day will show your birth and bring your
> ruin.

Jocasta implores:

> I beg you—do not hunt this out—I beg you,
> if you have any care for your own life.

Oedipus answers:

> I will not be persuaded to let be
> the chance of finding out the whole thing
> clearly.

Jocasta grows more frantic:

> O Oedipus, God help you!
> God keep you from the knowledge of who you are!

The old herdsman who saved the infant Oedipus when he was exposed by his parents to die on Mount Cithaeron tries not to reveal his knowledge, and tries to silence the messenger from Corinth who knows another part of the puzzle. When Oedipus finally forces him with threats of torture, the shepherd cries out:

> O God, I am on the brink of frightful speech.

and Oedipus answers resolutely:

> And I of frightful hearing. But I must hear.

If there is a bitter and desperate pride in that remark, it replaces a more carefree pride and arrogance—what the Greeks called *hubris*, transgression—earlier in the play. The first speech has Oedipus announce himself as:

> I Oedipus whom all men call the Great.

The priest who has come leading a chorus of suppliants addresses him:

> Now Oedipus, whom all men call the Greatest.

Later Oedipus boasts to Teiresias of the solving of the Sphinx's riddle that brought him the rule of Thebes:

> I solved the riddle by my wit alone.

After his tragic discovery, Oedipus abases himself as a sinner but loses none of his sense of self-importance. He tells the chorus:

> No man but I can bear my evil doom.

Going into exile, Oedipus informs Creon:

> Yet I know this much:
> no sickness and no other thing will kill me.
> I would not have been saved from death if not
> for some strange evil fate. Well, let my fate
> go where it will.

Creon's final advice to him, and the last words spoken in the play before the chorus' concluding moral, is:

> Do not seek to be master in everything,

Bernard M. W. Knox, in *Oedipus at Thebes*, has denied that any of this pride constitutes a flaw in Oedipus' character. "Oedipus is not a man guilty of a moral fault," he writes, and explains:

> The decisive actions are the product of an admirable character; with the possible exception of his anger (and even that springs initially from his devotion to the city), their source is the greatness and nobility of the man and the ruler.

Lane Cooper, it seems to me, in his introduction to *Ten Greek Plays*, has perceived the pattern more clearly. He writes:

> Young Oedipus kills an old man, whom he should have revered, in a dispute over the right of way, and thus unknowingly slays his own father. Unpremeditated murder, under provocation, was done in hot blood. Upon this act, which is anterior to the play, more light is thrown by the repeated bursts of anger from Oedipus, and particularly by his violence to old men, of whom this tragedy has a large share.

As Cooper suggests, the Oedipus who earlier killed Laius in a fit of passion is the Oedipus in the play who reviles old Teiresias and drives him away, sentences old Creon to death on suspicion of treason, and has the old herdsman tortured. He is a proper king in the Theban line, descended from the *Spartoi* or sown-men Cadmus raised from the serpent's teeth, with the lancehead mark of hot-headedness and violence on him.

The pervasive tone of the action in *Oedipus the King* is ironic. Early in the play Oedipus says to the priest:

> May I prove a villain,
> if I shall not do all the God commands.

When he takes on the quest for Laius' murderer, Oedipus announces to Creon:

> Whoever
> he was that killed the king may readily
> wish to dispatch me with his murderous hand;
> so helping the dead king I help myself.

Oedipus then formally curses the unknown murderer to banishment and misery. He adds rhetorically:

> If with my knowledge he lives at my hearth
> I pray that I myself may feel my curse.

He says of Laius:

> I fight in his defense as for my father.

Later in the play Jocasta triumphantly announces that Laius's murder by a stranger at a crossroads, when it had been prophesied that his son should kill him, is the refutation of oracles. Oedipus makes the same announcement when the messenger from Corinth tells him of the natural death of King Polybus, his adopted father, whom he believes to be his real father and the man he was prophesied to slay. The last words of the play, spoken by the Chorus, are the famous ironic injunction:

> Count no mortal happy till
> he has passed the final limit of his life secure
> from pain.

The texture of *Oedipus the King*, its language and metaphor, strongly reinforces its tragic and ironic action, and is in fact another dimension of the action. The basic metaphor of the play, one it shares with a number of other Greek tragedies, is the paradox of vision, the blindness of sight as opposed to the insight of blindness, and its chief metaphoric action is the bringing of what has been hidden into the light. In the play's first *agon* or contest, the abusive quarrel between Oedipus and Teiresias, Oedipus charges:

> You are blind in mind and ears
> as well as in your eyes.

and Teiresias answers:

> Since you have taunted me with being blind,
> here is my word for you.
> You have your eyes but see not where you are
> in sin, nor where you live, nor whom you live
> with.

When Oedipus first begins to suspect that he is the slayer of Laius (although not yet that he is Laius' son) he says to Jocasta:

> I have a deadly fear
> that the old seer had eyes.

To Jocasta later, Oedipus states his intention as "to bring my birth to light." When he finally learns the whole awful truth, he cries out:

> O, O, O, they will all come,
> all come out clearly! Light of the sun, let me
> look upon you no more after today!

When Oedipus finds Jocasta hanging dead, he tears the brooches from her robe and dashes out his eyes. He can finally "see" all.

Another dominant image that develops as a

strand of the play's action is the plague. In the first scene, the priest announces to Oedipus:

> A blight is on the fruitful plants of the earth,
> a blight is on the cattle in the fields,
> a blight is on your women that no children
> are born to them; a God that carries fire,
> a deadly pestilence, is on our town,
> strikes us and spares not, and the house of
> Cadmus
> is emptied of its people while black Death
> grows rich in groaning and in lamentation.

Here is the ancient Greek idea that murder, particularly regicide, pollutes the land, and underlying it the still more primitive idea that the life of the crops, the flocks, and human progeny is tied up with the life and health of the king. Creon tells Oedipus that his command from the oracle of Apollo is "to drive out a pollution from our land," and Oedipus' curse on the murderer is consequently:

> I forbid that man, whoever he be, my land,
> my land where I hold sovereignty and throne;
> and I forbid any to welcome him
> or cry him greeting or make him a sharer
> in sacrifice or offering to the Gods,
> or give him water for his hands to wash.
> I command all to drive him from their homes,
> since he is our pollution, as the oracle of
> Pytho's God proclaimed him now to me.

Provoked beyond endurance, Teiresias finally charges "*You* are the land's pollution." When a messenger brings the news of Jocasta's suicide to the chorus, he says, naming two great rivers, "Phasis nor Ister cannot purge this house." But in his description of Oedipus' blinding, he describes it like the great freeing of the waters in mythology:

> And the bleeding eyeballs gushed
> and stained his beard—no sluggish oozing drops
> but a black rain and bloody hail poured down.

In that blood of expiation pouring on the ground like fertilizing rain on the waste land, we know that Thebes will be cleansed of the blight.

In his invaluable book, no less invaluable for being occasionally wrong-headed, Knox has traced a great many structural and textural metaphors through the play: Oedipus as hunter, as pilot of the ship of state, as ploughman, as detective and prosecuting attorney. He concludes by making Oedipus a universal symbol: for man, the city, the whole Greek universe. "Oedipus is not only the questioner but also the answer to the question," Knox writes. "He is not only the revealer but also the thing revealed." Knox even finds the whole of the play's action implicit in puns buried in the hero's name and made on it.

Before our time the dominant interpretation of *Oedipus the King* was as a tragedy of fate or destiny. In recent years a vision of it as a psychological exploration, even a psychological mystery drama, has replaced the earlier interpretation. Grene's introduction to his translation remarks that "the mental processes of Oedipus prove to be correctly and profoundly studied." Freud named what he regarded as "the nuclear complex of the neuroses," the Oedipus complex, after the play's hero, and many a modern reader is inclined to see Sophocles as a premature Freudian in such lines as Jocasta's bland assurance to Oedipus:

> Before this, in dreams too, as well as oracles,
> many a man has lain with his own mother.

At a time when character and personality have become for us what fate and destiny were for the Greeks, it is useful to have Fergusson's reminder that the play is fundamentally a pattern of action, not character, and Knox's that it has so many strands of meaning that any essentializing interpretation is inevitably reductive.

Our B work or Poetics is naturally enough Aristotle's *Poetics*, a lecture composed about a century after *Oedipus the King*, approximately 330 B.C. We have the lecture only in the form of rough and incomplete notes, perhaps from Aristotle's hand, but more likely, because of the confusions, from one of his pupils. The surviving treatise deals primarily with tragedy and secondarily with epic, with comedy skimped and lyric poetry almost entirely ignored. I will quote it in Ingram Bywater's translation, confining myself to its remarks on tragedy.

However sparing one tries to be of Greek in addressing a general audience (and some of us in any case have little Greek to spare), five Greek words are necessary to Aristotle's definition of tragedy, or more properly, Aristotle's formula for tragedy. They are: *mimesis*, imitation; *hamartia*, the shortcoming or tragic flaw, which derives etymologically from missing the mark with an arrow, and means something like false-seeing or lack of insight; *peripeteia*, change of direction; *anagnorisis*, discovery; and *katharsis* or purging. In Aristotle's formula, tragedy is an imitation of an action in dramatic form and poetic language, serious and complete in itself. Ideally its protagonist is a man fundamentally good, whose *hamartia* is a failure of perception, and its plot is a complex one hinging on a discovery or recognition that changes his fortune from happiness to misery. The purpose of this dramatic imitation is to arouse pity and fear in the audience and thus accomplish the *katharsis* of those emotions.

It should be obvious that almost every word of this neatly fits Sophocles' *Oedipus the King*. If "the perfect plot" is a *mimesis* of a thoroughly tragic action, with the protagonist reduced to misery, what more complete misery than the pervasive guilty horror that leaves the incestuous Jocasta dead, and the incestuous and parricidal Oedipus blind, beggared and banished? Aristotle defines the ideal tragic character:

> There remains, then, the intermediate kind of personage, a man not pre-eminently virtuous and just, whose misfortune, however, is brought upon him not by vice and depravity, but by some error of judgement, of the number of those in the enjoyment of great reputation and prosperity; e.g. Oedipus, Thyestes, and the men of note of similar families.

He explains *peripeteia* and *anagnorisis:*

> A peripety is the change from one state of things within the play to its opposite of the kind described, and that too in the way we are saying, in the probable or necessary sequence of events; as it is for instance in *Oedipus*. Here the opposite state of things is produced by the messenger, who, coming to gladden Oedipus and to remove his fears as to his mother, reveals the secret of his birth. . . . The finest form of discovery is one attended by peripeties, like that which goes with the discovery in *Oedipus*.

He adds:

> The best of all discoveries, however, is that arising from the incidents themselves, when the great surprise comes about through a probable incident, like that in the *Oedipus* of Sophocles.

Aristotle says of *katharsis* (and here I shift to Lane Cooper's translation, which is clearer on this point):

> Pity is what we feel at a misfortune that is out of proportion to the faults of a man; and Fear is what we feel when misfortune comes upon one like ourselves.

Aristotle continues, in Bywater's language:

> The tragic fear and pity may be aroused by the spectacle; but they may also be aroused by the very structure and incidents of the play; which is the better way and shows the better poet. The plot in fact should be so framed that, even without seeing the things take place, he who simply hears the account of them shall be filled with horror and pity at the incidents; which is just the effect that the mere recital of the story in *Oedipus* would have on one.

In Aristotle's view, the finest tragedies are always based on the stories of some few houses, that of Oedipus among them, as either agents or sufferers in some deed of horror (Oedipus being both). He adds:

> The deed of horror may be done by the doer knowingly and consciously, as in the old poets, and in Medea's murder of her children in Euripides. Or he may do it, but in ignorance of his relationship, and discover that afterwards, as does the Oedipus in Sophocles.

Doing the deed in ignorance is, as we might expect, better, "the right way."

Everywhere Aristotle affirms *Oedipus the King* and its author as the standard. He says:

> The chorus too should be regarded as one of the actors; it should be an integral part of the whole, and take a share in the action, that which it has in Sophocles rather than in Euripides.

Aristotle insists:

> There should be nothing improbable among the actual incidents. If it is unavoidable, however, it should be outside the tragedy, like the improbability in the *Oedipus* of Sophocles.

(He explains later that he is referring to the hero's ignorance of the circumstances of Laius' death.) By the end of the *Poetics* it is obvious that Aristotle places *Oedipus the King* at the pinnacle of tragedy, as he places tragedy at the pinnacle of the poetic arts. As against epic, Aristotle says,

> the tragic imitation requires less space for the attainment of its end, which is a great advantage, since the more concentrated effect is more pleasurable than one with a large admixture of time to dilute it (consider the *Oedipus* of Sophocles, for instance, and the effect of ex-

panding it into the number of lines of the *Iliad*).

As this last quotation suggests, the aim of tragedy is pleasure or delight. It is natural for all of us to delight in works of imitation, Aristotle says, adding:

> Though the objects themselves may be painful to see, we delight to view the most realistic representations of them in art.

The specific tragic pleasure is that of pity and fear, and the arousing and purging of those emotions are assumed to be pleasurable in themselves. At the same time, tragedy ennobles its subjects, making its personages better than the men of its time. Aristotle quotes Sophocles' statement that "he drew men as they ought to be, and Euripides as they were." In purging the passions and focussing the audience's attention on ideal behavior, tragedy performs a valuable social function as well as furnishing pleasure to the individual, and the *Poetics* in one aspect is an argument with the contention of Aristotle's teacher Plato in his dialogue *The Republic* that poetry has anti-social effects. Sophocles is thus the purveyor of pleasure, morality, and improvement, or the beautiful, the true, and the good. Euripides is clearly nothing of the sort. Aristotle calls him "the most tragic, certainly, of the dramatists," for his unhappy endings, and has high praise for some of his discovery scenes, but suggests that his procedure is faulty in every other respect. In a critical world where *Oedipus the King* is the standard of dramatic construction, no play by Euripides can either improve or delight us.

We may take as our C example, or the CHALLENGE to the Aristotelian *poetics*, the *Medea* of Euripides. First performed in Athens in 431 B.C., about the time of *Oedipus the King*, it helped win Euripides a third prize. Our play tells the story of Medea's revenge against her husband Jason. When he deserts her to marry the daughter of Creon the ruler of Corinth, she slays Creon and his daughter with gifts magically poisoned, kills her two sons by Jason, and flies off through the sky to a promised asylum in Athens. I quote from *The Medea* in Rex Warner's translation.

In our day, H. D. F. Kitto has been the chief voice in calling to our attention the fact that Medea doesn't fit Aristotle's *Poetics*, or vice versa. Medea is not an Aristotelian tragic hero, he argues in *Greek Tragedy*, she is not someone like ourselves, a "character compounded of good and bad." Actually, it is more than a matter of the heroine. The whole play has little contact with the world of the *Poetics*. To begin with, there is the matter of making a woman the protagonist. Aristotle says of character in the *Poetics:*

> Such goodness is possible in every type of personage, even in a woman or a slave, though the one is perhaps an inferior, and the other a wholly worthless being. The second point is to make them appropriate. The character before us may be, say, manly; but it is not appropriate in a female character to be manly, or clever.

If women are perhaps inferior, weak and stupid in Aristotle's world, they are not any of those things in the world of Euripides' plays. Elsewhere Aristotle says of the agents of the action, or characters:

> It follows, therefore, that the agents represented must be either above our own level of goodness, or beneath it, or just such as we are.

Medea is not on any of those levels. As Kitto says, she is not a flawed mortal like us. She is not remotely comparable to us. She is a semi-divine witch, as remorseless and implacable as the gods, and as unanswerable as they to judgment in terms of "goodness."

Aristotle complains of the play's obvious improbability, the fortuitous appearance of Aegeus, the ruler of Athens and an old friend, in Corinth just when Medea needs a promise of asylum. "There is no possible apology for improbability of plot or depravity of character when they are not necessary and no use is made of them," Aristotle says firmly, finding this onstage improbability more unforgiveable than the offstage improbability in *Oedipus the King*. In a realistic world, true, it is highly improbable, but Medea's web of evil justice is not a realistic world, and if Euripides does not dramatize her arrival in Athens it is because Aegeus' Athens is a refuge of the tormented spirit, not a city fifty-three miles from Corinth. Aristotle's principal complaint, however, is not at the minor improbability of Aegeus' appearance, but at the play's ending, which he rightly sees as a violation of all his principles. The ending is probably, with the ending of Euripides' *Hecuba*, the most shocking and wonderful scene in Greek drama. After Medea has killed her sons, the audience sits breathlessly awaiting the *theophany*, the appearance of the god above the stage to administer justice, punish the guilty, and restore order. Instead, Medea herself appears above the stage, with the bloody corpses of her children in her arms, riding a chariot drawn by serpents given her by her grandfather the Sun, to taunt Jason and fly off to Athens.

Aristotle says curtly of this epiphany in glory: "The denouement should arise out of the plot itself, and not depend on a stage-artifice, as in *Medea*." The most untragic plot that can be, he remarked earlier, is the progress of a bad man (or woman, if we allow women to be tragic protagonists) from misery to happiness:

> It has no one of the requisites of tragedy; it does not appeal either to the human feeling in us, or to our pity, or to our fears.

Aristotle's word for "appealing to the human feeling in us" is *philanthropon*, "mankind-loving" or "consistent with the love of humanity." That is, such an epiphany or manifestation at the end is not only unjust, it is unnatural. A. W. Verrall neatly solved the problem for Aristotle around the turn of our century by announcing that the last scene of the *Medea* was no part of the original play, but was added for public performance. More sensibly, Kitto has written:

> Sun and Earth, the most elemental things in the universe, have been outraged by these terrible crimes; what will they do? how will they avenge their sullied purity? What Earth will do we shall not be told, but we are told what the Sun does: he sends a chariot to rescue the murderess.
>
> Is this illogical? Could anything be finer, more imaginative?

The primitive things in the universe, Kitto adds, are not reasonable:

> The magic chariot is a frightening glimpse of something that we shall see in full force in the *Bacchae*, the existence in the universe of forces

that we can neither understand nor control—only participate in.

The special tragic action of *Medea*, quite un-Aristotelian in conception, is Medea's revenge on those who scorned her. The nurse and the tutor begin the play by calling her (sensibly not to her face) "poor Medea," "poor creature," "poor fool." It is this poor scorned creature who appears in divine vengeance at the end, like Dionysus in *The Bacchae* or Hecuba in *Hecuba*. The motivation Medea repeatedly gives for her actions is that she will not be mocked. She rejects the idea of killing Creon and his daughter in person, since she might be caught "and give my enemies cause for laughter." She addresses herself in soliloquy:

> Never
> Shall you be mocked by Jason's Corinthian
> wedding.

Later, determining to kill the children: "For it is not bearable to be mocked by enemies." As the moment approaches she asks:

> Do I want to let go
> My enemies unhurt and be laughed at for it?

and answers:

> This shall never be, that I should suffer my
> children
> To be the prey of my enemies' insolence.

In the final scene, taunting Jason, she exclaims:

No, it was not to be that you should scorn
my love,
And pleasantly live your life through, laughing
at me.

The movement is thus, like that of *The Bacchae*, the mocker mocked, the persecutor persecuted, and the dramatic irony is very strong. In the great bitter *agon* between Jason and Medea, Jason's defense of his desertion is that he has more than repaid Medea with the inestimable blessings of Greek civilization and fame. He says:

But on this question of saving me, I can prove
You have certainly got from me more than
you gave.
Firstly, instead of living among barbarians,
You inhabit a Greek land and understand our
ways,
How to live by law instead of the sweet will of
force.
And all the Greeks considered you a clever
woman.
You were honored for it; while, if you were
living at
The ends of the earth, nobody would have
heard of you.

Medea's barbarian "sweet will of force" overcomes all of Greek law and moderation, and it is her terrible crime that brings her undying fame, as she recognizes more truly, telling the chorus:

Let no one think me a weak one, feeble-spirited,
A stay-at-home, but rather just the opposite,
One who can hurt my enemies and help my friends;
For the lives of such persons are most remembered.

Another violent irony builds to Medea's final epiphany in glory. When the messenger brings her news that Creon and his daughter are dead, he says:

Medea, you who have done such a dreadful thing,
So outrageous, run for your life, take what you can,
A ship to bear you hence or chariot on land.

Jason then explains to the chorus:

For she will have to hide herself beneath the earth,
Or raise herself on wings into the height of air,
If she wishes to escape the royal vengeance.

Despite the messenger, Medea needs neither ship on the sea nor chariot on land; Jason's rhetoric is ironically prophetic, and a divine chariot of the air, the Sun's own serpent-car, carries her away to safety.

One of the subtlest ironic suggestions in the play is that Medea is a kind of *maenad*, one of the divinely mad devotees of Dionysus whose rite of *sparagmos*, tearing apart the living flesh of the sacrifice, goes back to the primitive origins of Greek tragedy.

Before we ever see Medea onstage, the nurse describes her violent reaction to the news of Jason's wedding:

> Sometimes she twists back her white neck and
> Moans to herself.

This is the characteristic ecstatic posture of the *maenad*, and it is ironically echoed in the spiteful action of Creon's daughter when she sees Medea's sons, and turns her white neck scornfully away. A moment later daughter and father are the bleeding and dismembered sacrifice, slain by Medea's magic poisonous fire. The messenger tells us of the girl:

> From the top of
> Her head there oozed out blood and fire mixed together.
> Like the drops on pine-bark, so the flesh from her bones
> Dropped away, torn by the hidden fang of the poison.

When Creon falls upon the corpse in mourning, the poisoned dress clings to him, and his struggles to rise tear the flesh from his bones.

The movement of the action in the play is to a terrible doom that Medea, the other characters, and we the audience, all recognize as mad. In the first scene, the nurse warns:

> I am afraid she may think of some dreadful thing,
> For her heart is violent.

The nurse concludes with a hopeful wish:

> May it be an enemy and not a friend she hurts!

As soon as Medea appears, she delivers a general curse:

> I hate you,
> Children of a hateful mother. I curse you
> And your father. Let the whole house crash.

The chorus then warns the nurse:

> Hurry,
> Before she wrongs her own.
> This passion of hers moves to something great.

The nurse answers that grief is incurable,

> Bitter grief, from which death and disaster
> Cheat the hopes of a house.

During all the subsequent action, doom and madness are proclaimed by the chorus. When Medea finally learns that Creon's daughter has accepted the murderous gifts, she calls out in a revulsion of feeling:

> The gods and I,
> I in a kind of madness, have contrived all this.

After a violent dialogue with herself about killing the children, she concludes:

> I know indeed what evil I intend to do,
> But stronger than all my afterthoughts is my
> fury,

> Fury that brings upon mortals the greatest evils.

As she runs off the stage to murder her sons, Medea's last words are: "Oh, I am an unhappy woman."

Of the four types of madness Euripides' friend Socrates lists in the *Phaedrus* (or Plato lists for him) —prophetic, ritual, poetic, and erotic—this madness is erotic in its origins, ritual in its means, but ultimately it is the madness of *Erinys* and wild *Ate*, the madness of divine vengeance. Medea is the human instrument of the gods' vengeance, while at the same time she is herself enough divine, the Sun's granddaughter, to be executing her own vengeance, and she reminds Jason of the double authorship of his fate in the final episode. "When we remember that Medea was really a goddess," Gilbert Murray writes in his Excursus in Jane Harrison's *Themis*, "and that she and her children received worship in Greece, we can see that this [final] scene is really a faded or half-humanized Theophany."

The language of *Medea*, like that of *Oedipus the King*, powerfully reinforces its action, and provides much of the dramatic irony. Aristotle says in the *Poetics* that the older tragic poets had their protagonists speak like statesmen, whereas the newer tragedians have their protagonists speak like rhetoricians. The "rhetorician" charge has frequently been made against Euripides in Aristotle's name, although Aristotle apparently had only his own contemporaries in mind. There is no doubt that such speeches as

Jason's justification of his actions to Medea use the smooth and oily manner of the rhetorician, even to "firstly," "secondly," and "thirdly," but the use is deliberate and dramatic, to define character. In Medea's two great speeches, her reproach to Jason and her debate with herself over killing the children, she speaks with the elevation and transparently honest passion of a statesman, if a mad statesman.

The mocking and ironic word that runs all through the play is "love," in various forms of the root words *philia*, affectionate love, and *eros*, sexual love. The nurse opens the play by talking of Medea's "passionate love" for Jason, which is *eros*. The tutor explains Jason's behavior with "everyone loves himself more than his neighbor," which is *philia*. The nurse calls the children "*philoi*," darlings, and the chorus speaks of "The house I have loved so well," *philia* again. Medea bitterly complains, "Oh what an evil to men is passionate love!," *eros* once more. Later when the messenger reports the deaths of Creon and his daughter to Medea, she replies:

> Now and hereafter
> I shall count you among my benefactors and
> friends.

Philoi again. Jason, who had earlier in his self-defensive speech said that he was to her "the best of friends," *megas philos*, can at the end of the play only cry out "Oh, children I love!," *philtata*, an intensive. Thus to the sounds of "love, love, love," the play enacts its story of hate and betrayal. Similarly there is an ironic "joy" running through the action. Medea's Judas kiss, when she is trying to delay Creon's sentence of banishment from Corinth in order to destroy him and his daughter, is the blessing:

> May the marriage be a lucky one!

Aegeus greets her at her low point with the conventional "*Chaire*," joy. The princess receives the treacherous gifts "with joy." In her great debate with herself over killing the children, Medea twice calls out "*Chaireto*," farewell, to her murderous plans, before succumbing to them. In *Euripides and His Age*, Murray explains why the last scene of the anonymous play *Rhesus* makes him attribute it to Euripides. He writes:

> The poetry of the scene is exquisite; but what is most characteristic is the sudden flavour of bitterness, the cold wind that so suddenly takes the heart out of joyous war. Some touch of that bitter flavour will be found hereafter in every play, however beautiful or romantic, that comes from the pen of Euripides.

"Love" and "joy" here are the Euripidean hallmark, the characteristic flavor of bitterness, and if Jason is loveless and joyless at the end, so, despite her triumph, is Medea. The cold wind has taken the heart not only out of protagonist and antagonist, but out of the audience's blithe Aristotelian "philanthropism" too.

THE Greek critical treatise, of unknown date and authorship, that has come down to us as *Longinus on the Sublime*, is the D work or SANCTION for *Medea*. Addressed to a Roman friend, Postumius Terentianus, it was written during the Roman period, and from internal evidence is probably of the first or second centuries A.D. Let us compromise at about 100 A.D., more than five hundred years after *Medea* was written. The anonymous author, whom for convenience we will call "Longinus," as everyone does, analyzes the factors that make up sublimity or elevation in literature and lists the faults to be avoided, with a wealth of illustration and quotation. I quote from *Longinus on the Sublime* in the translation of W. Rhys Roberts.

Since it is my argument that Longinus finally rescues *Medea* from Aristotle's strictures and erects criteria that allows it to be a tragedy and a great one, it should in fairness be noted that the work never mentions *Medea*. More than that, Longinus disliked Euripides. He refers to him as one of those poets "who possess no natural sublimity and are perhaps even wanting in elevation," a poet "in virtue of his power of composition rather than of his invention." Longinus grants Euripides sublimity only grudgingly, since he believes that Euripides achieves it by artifice rather than by nature. Longinus writes:

> Now Euripides is most assiduous in giving the utmost tragic effect to those two emotions, fits of love and madness. Herein he succeeds more, perhaps, than in any other respect, although he is daring enough to invade all the other regions of the imagination. Notwithstanding that he is by nature anything but elevated, he forces his own genius in many passages to tragic heights; and everywhere in the matter of sublimity it is true of him, to adopt Homer's words, that
>
> The tail of him scourgeth his ribs and
> his flanks to left and to right,
> And he lasheth himself into frenzy, and
> spurreth him on to the fight.

Longinus' favorite playwright, like Aristotle's, seems to be Sophocles, but it is a very different Sophocles: the creator of the magnificent images of the death of Oedipus in *Oedipus at Colonus*, an author of rich and disorderly abundance showing "that outburst of the divine spirit within him which it is difficult to bring under the rules of law."

Despite Longinus' opinion of Euripides and his ignoring of the *Medea*, *Longinus on the Sublime* finally creates a critical emphasis that can accommodate the Euripidean extreme. Its vision of the tragic effect is not of *katharsis* but of rapture. In the introductory section, Longinus writes:

> The effect of elevated language upon an audience is not persuasion but transport. At every time and in every way imposing speech, with the spell it throws over us, prevails over that which aims at persuasion and gratification. Our persuasions we can usually control; but the influences of the sublime bring power and irresistible might to bear, and reign supreme over every hearer. Similarly we see skill in invention, and due order and arrangement of matter, emerging as the hard-won result not of one thing nor of two, but of the whole texture of the composition, whereas Sublimity flashing forth at the right moment scatters everything before it like a thunderbolt, and at once displays the power of the orator in its plenitude.

This emphasis on transport (*ekstasis*) and vehemence (*enthousiasmos*) is the attenuated successor to the old ritual possession in which the god entered into the worshipper and made him divine, as Longinus' metaphors make clear. He writes:

> For many men are carried away by the spirit of others as if inspired, just as it is related of the Pythian priestess when she approaches the tripod, where there is a rift in the ground which, they say, exhales divine vapour. By heavenly

> power thus communicated she is impregnated and straightway delivers oracles in virtue of the afflatus.

As with the Pythian priestess, "the design of the poetical image is enthralment."

The two most important components of the sublime, both "for the most part innate," are "the power of forming great conceptions" and "vehement and inspired passion." Longinus concludes that section of his treatise with the eloquent statement:

> I would affirm with confidence that there is no tone so lofty as that of genuine passion, in its right place, when it bursts out in a wild gust of mad enthusiasm, and as it were fills the speaker's words with frenzy.

Sappho, Longinus writes, demonstrates her supreme excellence "in the skill with which she selects and binds together the most striking and vehement circumstances of passion." "The great opportunity of Demosthenes' high-pitched elevation," he writes, "comes where intense utterance and vehement passion are in question, and in passages in which the audience is to be utterly enthralled." If there is a danger of overdoing the boldness and frequency of metaphors, "strong and timely passion and noble sublimity are the appropriate palliatives."

With all this intensity and passion, it is not surprising that Longinus accepts the utmost tragic effect of fits of love and madness as achieving the sublime. Here, in short, is the sanction for *Medea* as a great poem, whether Longinus mentions it or not. Furthermore, it is, for ancient literary criticism, a romantic revolution, and a romantic revolution against the classicism of Aristotle. Longinus writes:

> For some passions are found which are far removed from sublimity and are of a low order, such as pity, grief, and fear.

To Aristotle's classic slogans of order, discipline, moderation, control, Longinus opposes the very different slogans we will see again in the romantic nineteenth century. Life "everywhere abounds in what is striking, and great, and beautiful," he writes:

> This is why, by a sort of natural impulse, we admire not the small streams, useful and pellucid though they be, but the Nile, the Danube or the Rhine, and still more the Ocean. Nor do we view the tiny flame of our own kindling, guarded in lasting purity as its light ever is, with greater awe than the celestial fires though they are often shrouded in darkness; nor do we deem it a greater marvel than the craters of Etna, whose eruptions throw up stones from its depths and great masses of rock, and at times pour forth rivers of that pure and unmixed subterranean fire.

What could be more Shelleyan, we comment, and wonder why the eighteenth century found *Longi-*

nus on the Sublime so attractive. Dryden, Addison, Goldsmith, and Gibbon praised it highly, and Pope wrote in *Essay on Criticism:*

> Thee, bold Longinus! all the Nine inspire,
> And bless their critic with a poet's fire.
>
> Whose own example strengthens all his laws;
> And is himself the great sublime he draws.

It is not the last time we will see both parties quoting the same sacred book, although usually different texts from it. Thus Aristotle and Longinus both esteemed Sophocles, but reduced him to different qualities, and both shared a disrespect for Euripides, although one did his best to exclude him from the tragic canon, and the other canonized him as the tragedian of tragedians for centuries.

II

English Neo-Classicism

THE STANDARD OR A work for the English seventeenth century we will take to be a play by William Shakespeare, *The Tragedy of Antony and Cleopatra.* Written and produced about 1608, it was not published until the First Folio in 1623. *Antony and Cleopatra* covers twelve days, spread over ten years, in the downfall of Mark Antony, one of the rulers of the Roman world. In the course of the action he makes several unsuccessful efforts to leave Cleopatra and restore his imperial fortunes, even to marrying Octavia, the sister of his rival Octavius Caesar, after the death of his wife Fulvia. By the end of the play Antony's forces have been decisively defeated by Octavius', he has killed himself by falling on his sword, and Cleopatra has killed herself by means of poisonous serpents. Shakespeare's source is Plutarch's *Life of Antonius* in Thomas North's translation, and he follows its incidents with considerable fidelity and uses quite a bit of North's language.

The unredeemed gloominess of the events of the play I have just synopsized is counterpointed by the play's more significant action, which consists of a number of overcomings or transcendences so substantial that the play ends in a mood of triumph and exaltation rather than defeat. The most important of these transcendences is probably the victory of the spiritual value embodied in true love over the material things of the world. Early in the play Antony is a somewhat gross soldier enmeshed by his own sensuality, and Cleopatra an aging charmer not remarkable for emotional stability. By the end of the play, all their weaknesses and ambitions have been burned away by the events, and they are left the purified symbols of intense and triumphant passion. In the fourth act, believing Cleopatra dead, Antony prepares to die. Calling to her, Antony simultaneously calls to his attendant Eros who is to come and dispatch him with a sword, and Shakespeare takes advantage of the name he found in Plutarch to make the speech something like an apostrophe jointly to Cleopatra and to the god of love:

Eros!—I come, my queen. Eros! Stay for me.
Where souls do couch on flowers, we'll hand in
hand,

And with our sprightly port make the ghosts
gaze:
Dido and her Aeneas shall want troops,
And all the haunt be ours. Come, Eros! Eros!

The fifth act, with Antony dead, is given over to Cleopatra's spiritual transcendence. Resolved to die, Cleopatra says to Octavius' man Dolabella: "I dreamt there was an Emperor Antony." She continues:

His face was as the heavens, and therein stuck
A sun and moon, which kept their course and
lighted
The little O, th'earth. . . .
His legs bestrid the ocean; his rear'd arm
Crested the world: his voice was propertied
As all the tuned spheres, and that to friends;
But when he meant to quail and shake the orb,
He was as rattling thunder. For his bounty,
There was no winter in't; an Antony it was
That grew the more by reaping: his delights
Were dolphinlike, they show'd his back above
The element they liv'd in: in his livery
Walk'd crown and crownets; realms and is-
lands were
As plates dropp'd from his pocket.

In her final speeches, she transcends every element of the earlier Cleopatra: her gender ("I have nothing of woman in me"); her inconstancy ("I am marble-constant: now the fleeting moon/ No planet is of mine"); her role as mistress ("Husband, I come"); her earthiness ("I am fire and air; my other elements/ I give to baser life"); all her strivings ("Peace, peace! / Dost thou not see my baby at my breast,/ That sucks the nurse asleep?"). Octavius Caesar's final speeches over her body continue and complete the transcendence. She has overcome: her sin ("She looks like sleep,/ As she would catch another Antony/ In her strong toil of grace"); her isolation ("She shall be buried by her Antony"); and defeat ("Their story is/ No less in pity than his glory which/ Brought them to be lamented."). In *Shakespeare's Imagery, and What It Tells Us*, Caroline Spurgeon observes:

> The group of images in Antony and Cleopatra which, on analysis, immediately attracts attention as peculiar to this play, consists of images of the world, the firmament, the ocean and vastness generally. That is the dominating note in the play, magnificence and grandeur, expressed in many ways. . . .

She adds:

> This vastness of scale is kept constantly before us by the use of the word 'world,' which occurs forty-two times, nearly double, or more than double, as often as in most other plays, and it is continually employed in a way which increases the sense of grandeur, power and space,

> and which fills the imagination with the conception of beings so great that physical size is annihilated and the whole habitable globe shrinks in comparison with them.

G. Wilson Knight, in his remarkable essays on the play in *The Imperial Theme*, explains the function of the imagery:

> Empire-imagery throughout serves at least a dual purpose: suggesting both the material magnificence which Antony loses, and shadowing symbolically the finer spiritual magnificence of love for which he sacrifices it.

Another important overcoming in the play's action is that of loyalty over betrayal. In the first two acts of the play, Antony repudiates any attachment to Cleopatra. When she flees the battle of Actium in her ship, Antony nevertheless flies after her. Enobarbus, Antony's faithful officer, then announces:

> I'll yet follow
> The wounded chance of Antony, though my reason
> Sits in the wind against me.

Enobarbus later gives what is in effect the larger moral:

> Mine honesty and I begin to square.
> The loyalty well held to fools does make
> Our faith mere folly: yet he that can endure

To follow with allegiance a fall'n lord,
Does conquer him that did his master conquer.
And earns a place i' the' story.

When he sees Cleopatra apparently desert to Caesar, Enobarbus apostrophizes Antony ironically:

Sir, sir, thou art so leaky,
That we must leave thee to thy sinking, for
Thy dearest quit thee.

In fury at Cleopatra's apparent betrayal, Antony falls to his lowest point as a feudal master, who owes loyalty and service to his men as they owe it to him. He has Caesar's messenger whipped, and sends him to his master with the message:

If he mislike
My speech and what is done, tell him he has
Hipparchus, my enfranched bondman, whom
He may at pleasure whip, or hang, or torture,
As he shall like, to quit me.

When Cleopatra convinces Antony that she has been loyal he regains his joy and optimism, now unrealistically, and on that evidence Enobarbus finally decides to desert. He says in soliloquy:

I see still,
A diminution in our captain's brain
Restores his heart. When valor preys on reason
It eats the sword it fights with. I will seek
Some way to leave him.

Antony calls his servants together for a final feast, takes their hands, and affirms the feudal loyalty he had earlier betrayed:

> Perchance tomorrow
> You'll serve another master. I look on you
> As one that takes his leave. Mine honest friends,
> I turn you not away, but like a master
> Married to your good service, stay till death.

The next morning, when Antony is told that Enobarbus has deserted to Caesar's camp, he sends Enobarbus' chests and treasure to him with the message:

> Say that I wish he never find more cause
> To change a master. O, my fortunes have
> Corrupted honest men!

Shamed at Antony's generosity and his own betrayal, Enobarbus kills himself in Caesar's camp. Knowing now what place he has earned in the story, he says as his last words:

> O Antony!
> Nobler than my revolt is infamous
> Forgive me in thine own particular,
> But let the world rank me in register
> A master leaver and a fugitive.
> O Antony! O Antony!

The Enobarbus subplot has played out disloyalty and repentance, and the lovers, thus exorcised, conquer their mutual suspicions and die triumphantly loyal to each other.

Another victory in the play's action consists of the values clustered around "Egypt" overcoming those clustered around "Rome." When Antony and Cleopatra are disturbed, each turns destructively on his own place. Early in the play, baited by Cleopatra, Antony proclaims:

> Let Rome in Tiber melt, and the wide arch
> Of the rang'd empire fall! Here is my space.

When Cleopatra learns of Antony's marriage to Octavia, she cries out:

> Melt Egypt into Nile! and kindly creatures
> Turn all to serpents!

In the course of the play's action, Rome dissociates into its unlovely features, identified with Octavius Caesar, and its traditional virtues, embodied in Antony, so that he fights and dies "the firm Roman." At the same time, Cleopatra becomes "great Egypt," embodied as the "serpent of old Nile," and in the scene of her death by the asp, becomes herself an asp, hissing that "great Caesar" is "ass unpolicied." In the development of the images of Egypt and Rome, Egypt becomes a cluster of richness, fertility, excess, represented by Cleopatra, and Rome something poor, barren, and miserly, represented by Octavius, with Antony then naturally choosing Egypt.

The play begins in Alexandria on a denial of measure. Cleopatra enters saying:

> If it be love indeed, tell me how much.

Antony replies:

> There's beggary in the love that can be reck-
> on'd.

When he is married to Octavia, Antony turns to affirming measure and moderation. He says to her:

> I have not kept my square, but that to come
> Shall all be done by th' rule.

His faith in Cleopatra renewed, and resolved to fight valiantly the next day and die, Antony calls for feasting in characteristic terms:

> Come,
> Let's have one other gaudy night: call to me
> All my sad captains; fill our bowls once more:
> Let's mock the midnight bell.

Opposed to this is the petty shopkeeper Caesar, who calls for a feasting of his army at the same time in very different terms:

> And feast the army; we have store to do't,
> And they have earn'd the waste.

The imagery for the Egyptian cluster of values is not only lavishness and immoderation, but a lush and teeming fertility, amoral rather than immoral. In the first act, in a bawdy scene with the soothsayer, Cleopatra's attendants, Charmian and Iras, pun and joke endlessly on sexuality and fertility. When Charmian asks the soothsayer how many children she will have, he answers:

If every of your wishes had a womb,
And fertile every wish, a million.

When Iras says that her palm presages chastity, Charmian answers: "E'en as the o'erflowing Nilus presageth famine." When Charmian asks Iras where, if she had an extra inch of fortune, she would choose it, Iras answers: "Not in my husband's nose," and Charmian comments "Our worser thoughts Heavens mend!" The sexual imagery that Shakespeare did not need Freud to discover for him abounds in the play. When Antony swears "By my sword," Cleopatra adds "And target." She sends him off to the wars with the Freudian blessing:

Upon your sword
Sit laurel victory.

In the great description, following Plutarch, that Enobarbus gives of Cleopatra's first appearance to Antony, her sexuality is so overpowering that it imbues the entire scene. He says:

The barge she sat in, like a burnish'd throne
Burnt on the water: the poop was beaten gold,
Purple the sails, and so perfumed that
The winds were lovesick with them; the oars were silver,
Which to the tune of flutes kept stroke, and made
The water which they beat to follow faster,
As amorous of their strokes.

In a magnificently bold metaphor, even the barge's ropes become sexually stimulated:

The silken tackle
Swell with the touches of those flower-soft hands
That yarely frame the office.

When Antony is away from Cleopatra, she asks the messenger for news of him in explicitly sexual terms:

Ram thou thy fruitful tidings in mine ears,
That long time have been barren.

Cleopatra's terrible rhetorical curses on herself have the same teeming fertility, put now in horror terms. To convince Antony, she asks to be struck by poison hail,

Till by degrees the memory of my womb,
Together with my brave Egyptians all,
By the discandying of this pelleted storm,
Lie graveless, till the flies and gnats of Nile
Have buried them for prey!

After his death, she states a preferred alternative to being led to Rome in triumph by Caesar:

Rather a ditch in Egypt
Be gentle grave unto me! rather on Nilus' mud
Lay me stark nak'd, and let the water flies
Blow me into abhorring!

The scene that precedes Cleopatra's dignified and moving death is a scene of coarse clowning from the rustic who brings the serpents, playing endless variations on his one phallic joke. His farewell, "I wish you joy o' th' worm," introduces the death scene with an indescribable poignancy, merging sex and death, sadness and joy, so that Cleopatra dies in a true *Liebestod*, overcoming all the superficially-victorious Roman barrenness and sterility.

As Cleopatra eventually becomes identified with the teeming womb of Egypt, the overflowing Nile and its fertile mud, so Antony becomes some great phallic monument, and his death an event like the extinction of virility. After his final defeat, as he prepares to die, he proclaims, "This pine is bark'd,/ That overtopp'd them all." At the moment of his death, Cleopatra mourns the end of all mature sexuality:

> The crown o' th' earth doth melt. My lord!
> O, wither'd is the garland of the war,
> The soldier's pole is fall'n: young boys and
> girls
> Are level now with men.

The play's ultimate transcendent action, one that embraces all the others, is a mingling or melting together of all separateness, as Knight has shown. "O heavenly mingle!" Cleopatra calls Antony. All the elements merge as the play progresses. Before the first battle, Antony debated whether to fight at land or sea, but before the second:

I would they'ld fight i' th' fire or i' th' air;
We'ld fight there too.

Antony sums it all up in his touching speech to Eros, just before they die, on the illusory images in clouds and how all visible outlines melt away and become indistinct, "as water is in water." Cleopatra in turn sums it up, just before *she* dies, in her speech to Dolabella on her dream of a cosmic Antony. By the end of the play, all reality, all substance, has been dissolved and merged into one "great solemnity," a dream more real than the real world.

As the play's action is a series of transcendences, rather than a simple Aristotelian fall or rise, so its characters show depths of complex humanity richer than anything in Greek drama. Antony begins the play as a passive victim, proclaiming:

These strong Egyptian fetters I must break,
Or lose myself in dotage.

and

I must from this enchanting queen break off.

He ultimately renounces power and glory out of love, no longer passively fettered or enchanted, but actively choosing his fate. Cleopatra begins the play a volatile tease. She sends Alexas to Antony:

If you find him sad,
Say I am dancing; if in mirth, report
That I am sudden sick.

As the play continues, this becomes more and more a godlike attribute. Enobarbus says of her, in a famous tribute:

Age cannot wither her, nor custom stale
Her infinite variety: other women cloy
The appetites they feed, but she makes hungry
Where most she satisfies.

Cleopatra's low point is the scene where she curses and sadistically threatens the messenger who has brought her news of Antony's marriage to Octavia, but Shakespeare brilliantly recovers her dignity in the last lines:

Pity me, Charmian,
But do not speak to me. Lead me to my chamber.

In another famous passage, Cleopatra excuses her youthful dalliance with Julius Caesar in the imagery of food:

My salad days,
When I was green in judgment, cold in blood.

When Antony is most furious with her, he charges:

I found you as a morsel, cold upon
Dead Caesar's trencher.

By the end of the play she has become, in the rustic's words, "a dish for the gods."

The other characters come alive comparably. Enobarbus, the cynical soldier, reveals a hidden sensibility, in his grudging description of Cleopatra's magic, which later pours out eloquently at his death. Octavius shows us his heart twice, and both times it reveals a boyish hero-worship for Antony and a strong love that, scorned, turned on him destructively. The first time, told of Pompey's threat to their triumvirate, he addresses the absent Antony touchingly:

> Antony,
> Leave thy lascivious wassails.

and continues with a long reminiscence of Antony's heroism and hardihood as a warrior. The second time is when he hears of Antony's death, and again apostrophizes him:

> O Antony!
> I have follow'd thee to this.

At the end of the deeply moving speech, the mask is put back on abruptly, and Caesar returns to his usual tone and begins to prepare an apology to show "How hardly I was drawn into this war," and that everything was Antony's fault. A. C. Bradley writes in *Oxford Lectures on Poetry*, of Octavius:

> To Shakespeare he is one of those men, like Bolingbroke and Ulysses, who have plenty of 'judgment' and not much 'blood.' Victory in the world, according to the poet, almost always goes to such men; and he makes us respect, fear, and dislike them.

Things are somewhat more ambivalent than that. Octavius has lots of passion, carefully repressed, and it is this curdled love that destroys Antony.

The language and metaphor of the play, fitting its action and character, is indescribably splendid. Recalling their earlier love, Cleopatra says to Antony:

> Eternity was in our lips and eyes,
> Bliss in our brows' bent.

In a line that would have pleased Longinus, the sentry says when Enobarbus' suicide is discovered:

> The hand of death hath raught him.

After his attempt at suicide, Antony says to Cleopatra:

> I am dying, Egypt, dying; only
> I here importune death awhile.

The effect of the long Latinate word "importune" here, with the short Anglo-Saxon words, shows Shakespeare's mastery of language perhaps better than any other example. For his mastery of effect, we need only note the last words of Charmian, who survives Cleopatra and Iras by a moment. As the guardsman breaks in and protests, Charmian says as she dies:

> It is well done, and fitting for a princess
> Descended of so many royal kings.
> Ah, soldier.

In their combination of solemnity and the unquenchable passion of the young and fair, these lines themselves are unimaginably fitting and well done.

THERE is no B work or POETICS that erects Shakespeare or *Antony and Cleopatra* into the standard in the seventeenth century. We know that the century accepted Shakespeare as the greatest of dramatists with hardly a dissent, but the literary criticism of most of the period ignored the drama and concerned itself with other literature. Two outstanding poet-critics, Ben Jonson and John Milton, praised Shakespeare highly in the first third of the century, but both tributes are in verse, and neither is lengthy enough to constitute a poetics. Such a work was in fact not written in England until the nineteenth century, when Coleridge, Hazlitt and others finally did for Shakespeare what Aristotle had done for Sophocles, made his writing the standard of what the greatest writing should be. We are forced, therefore, to construct a composite poetics from what contemporary discussions are available. Most of these are reprinted in D. Nichol Smith's *Shakespeare Criticism: A Selection.*

In the sheaf of tributes printed in the First Folio of Shakespeare's plays in 1623, two are of critical importance. The first is by John Heminge and Henry Condell, the editors. They write:

> Who, as he was a happie imitator of Nature, was a most gentle expresser of it. His mind and hand went together. What he thought, he uttered with that easinesse, that wee have scarse received from him a blot in his papers.

Here, in three sentences, is the heart of the century's view of Shakespeare. He imitated nature and wrote by nature rather than art, with the fluency of natural expression. Furthermore, this artlessness is not apologized for, but accepted as the highest literary quality.

The other important tribute in the First Folio is Ben Jonson's famous poem, "To the memory of my beloved, The Author Mr. William Shakespeare: and what he hath left us." Jonson begins:

> To draw no envy (Shakespeare) on thy name,
> Am I thus ample to thy Booke, and Fame:
> While I confesse thy writings to be such,
> As neither Man, nor Muse, can praise too much.

He goes on to call him:

> Soule of the Age!
> The applause! delight! the wonder of our Stage!

After listing the English dramatists Shakespeare outshone, Jonson continues:

And though thou hadst small Latine, and less
Greeke,
From thence to honour thee, I would not
seeke
For names; but call forth thund'ring Aeschilus,
Euripides, and Sophocles to us.

"He was not for an age, but for all time!," Jonson adds. He explains:

Nature her self was proud of his designes,
And joy'd to weare the dressing of his lines!
Which were so richly spun, and woven so fit,
As, since, she will vouchsafe no other Wit.

So far, in accord with Heminge and Condell. Then Jonson adds:

Yet must I not give Nature all: Thy Art,
My gentle Shakespeare, must enjoy a part.
For though the Poets matter, Nature be,
His Art doth give the fashion. And, that he,
Who casts to write a living line, must sweat,
(Such as thine are) and strike the second
heat
Upon the Muses anvile: turne the same,
(And himselfe with it) that he thinkes to
frame;
Or for the lawrell, he may gaine a scorne,
For a good Poet's made, as well as borne.
And such wert thou.

After praising Shakespeare's "well turned, and true-filed lines" and calling him "Sweet Swan of Avon,"

Jonson concludes by transferring him to the heavens as a constellation, the star of poets. In these final statements, Jonson defines his minority view in the century; not only the genius of natural expression, but art, sweat, turning and filing, all that we call the *craft* of poetry.

The other tributes in the First Folio need not much concern us. Hugh Holland calls Shakespeare "Poets King" and says his lines will be immortal, Leonard Digges says his "wit-fraught Booke" will assure his immortality, "crown'd with Lawrell," and I. M. says prettily that he has only briefly gone offstage to reenter to applause. Essentially, both the terms of poetic greatness are complete in Heminge and Condell and Jonson: easy nature and hard art.

The Second Folio of 1632 primarily develops the first term. Milton's "Epitaph" says:

Thou in our wonder and astonishment
Hast built thy self a live-long Monument.
For whilst to th' shame of slow-endeavouring
 art,
Thy easie numbers flow, and that each heart,
Hath from the leaves of thy unvalu'd Book,
Those Delphick lines with deep impression
 took, . . .

("Unvalu'd" is of course invaluable, not valueless.) A longer verse tribute by the anonymous I. M. S., "On Worthy Master Shakespeare and his Poems," emphasizes Shakespeare's ability to bring the past to life and to move an audience. I. M. S. writes:

A Mind reflecting ages past, whose cleere
And equall surface can make things appeare
Distant a Thousand yeares, and represent
Them in their lively colours just extent.

Opposed to "what Poets faine/ At second hand," is Shakespeare's ability

To give a Stage
(Ample and true with life) voyce, action, age.

I. M. S. continues:

To raise our auncient Soveraignes from their
herse
Make Kings his subjects, by exchanging verse
Enlive their pale trunkes, that the present age
Joyes in their joy, and trembles at their rage:
Yet so to temper passion, that our eares
Take pleasure in their paine; And eyes in teares
Both weepe and smile; fearefull at plots so sad,
Then laughing at our feare; abus'd, and glad
To be abus'd, affected with that truth
Which we perceive is false; pleas'd in that ruth
At which we start; and by elaborate play
Tortur'd and tickled: by a crablike way
Time past made pastime, and in ugly sort
Disgorging up his ravaine for our sport . . .
Now to move
A chilling pitty, then a rigorous love:
To strike up and stroake downe, both joy and
ire;

To steere th' affections; and by heavenly fire
Mould us anew.

In addition to the tributes in the Folios, a few other statements are significant. In a poem prefixed to the 1640 edition of Shakespeare's *Poems*, Leonard Digges reported the enthusiasm of audiences for Shakespeare in comparison with Jonson:

So have I seene, when Cesar would appeare,
And on the Stage at halfe-sword parley were
Brutus and Cassius: oh how the Audience
Were ravish'd, with what wonder they went thence,
When some new day they would not brooke a line
Of tedious (though well laboured) Catiline;
Sejanus too was irkesome, they priz'de more
Honest Iago, or the jealous Moore.

And so on. The following year, perhaps nettled by the comparison, Jonson published a prose comment on Shakespeare in *Timber: or, Discoveries*, somewhat more critical and ambivalent than his poem in the First Folio. Picking up Heminge and Condell, Jonson writes:

I remember, the Players have often mentioned it as an honour to Shakespeare, that in his writing, (whatsoever he penn'd) hee never blotted out line. My answer hath beene, would he had blotted a thousand. Which they thought a malevolent speech. I had not told posterity

> this, but for their ignorance, who choose that circumstance to commend their friend by, wherein he most faulted. And to justifie mine owne candor, (for I lov'd the man, and doe honour his memory (on this side Idolatry) as much as any.) Hee was (indeed) honest, and of an open, and free nature: had an excellent Phantsie; brave notions, and gentle expressions: wherein hee flow'd with that facility, that sometime it was necessary he should be stop'd.

"His wit was in his owne power," Jonson adds, "would the rule of it had beene so too." He concludes:

> But hee redeemed his vices, with his vertues. There was ever more in him to be praysed then to be pardoned.

In this perhaps annoyed, but more candid and less eulogistic statement, Jonson puts the issue more clearly. If poetry is the facility of genius and the pains of rewriting, in Jonson's view Shakespeare had the facility without taking enough of the pains.

In 1662, Thomas Fuller's *The History of the Worthies of England* was published, a year after Fuller's death. In it Fuller developed Heminge and Condell's view, to which Jonson had come around, of Shakespeare as an unstudied natural. He writes:

> He was an eminent instance of the truth of that Rule, *Poeta non fit, sed nascitur*, one is not *made* but *born* a Poet. Indeed his Learning was

very little, so that as Cornish diamonds are not polished by any Lapidary, but are pointed and smoothed even as they are taken out of the Earth, so *nature* it self was all the *art* which was used upon him.

Many were the wit-combates betwixt him and Ben Johnson, which two I behold like a a Spanish great Gallion, and an English man of War; Master Johnson (like the former) was built far higher in Learning; Solid, but Slow in his performances. Shake-spear with the English-man of War, lesser in bulk, but lighter in sailing, could turn with all tides, tack about and take advantage of all winds, by the quickness of his Wit and Invention.

In 1664, the *Sociable Letters* of Margaret Cavendish, Marchioness of Newcastle, were published. One of them, a defense of Shakespeare to a friend, brings a new term, universality, into the discussion. She writes:

Yet Shakespear did not want Wit, to Express to the Life all Sorts of Persons, of what Quality, Profession, Degree, Breeding, or Birth soever; nor did he want Wit to Express the Divers, and Different Humours, or Natures, or Several Passions in Mankind; and so Well he hath Express'd in his Playes all Sorts of Persons, as one would think he had been Transformed into every one of those Persons he hath Described; and as sometimes one would think he was Really

> himself the Clown or Jester he Feigns, so one would think, he was also the King, and Privy Counsellor also as one would think he were Really the Coward he Feigns, so one would think he were the most Valiant, and Experienced Souldier; Who would not think he had been such a man as his Sir John Falstaff? and who would not think he had been Harry the Fifth? & certainly Julius Caesar, Augustus Caesar, and Antonius, did never Really Act their parts Better, if so Well, as he hath Described them, and I believe that Antonius and Brutus did not Speak Better to the People, than he hath Feign'd them; nay, one would think that he had been Metamorphosed from a Man to a Woman, for who could Describe Cleopatra Better than he hath done, and many other Females of his own Creating.

Lady Cavendish continues:

> And in his Tragick Vein, he Presents Passions so Naturally, and Misfortunes so Probably, as he Peirces the Souls of his Readers with such a True Sense and Feeling thereof, that it Forces Tears through their Eyes, and almost Perswades them, they are Really Actors, or at least Present at those Tragedies. Who would not Swear he had been a Noble Lover, that could Woo so well? and there is not any person he hath Described in his Book, but his Readers might think they were well acquainted with

> them; indeed Shakespear had a Clear Judgment, a Quick Wit, a Spreading Fancy, a Subtil Observation, a Deep Apprehension, and a most Eloquent Elocution; truly, he was a Natural Orator, as well as a Natural Poet.

In 1675, Edward Phillips, Milton's nephew, published in *Theatrum Poetarum* a brief account of Shakespeare that developed the earlier image of Shakespeare as an untutored natural genius into some sort of wild native growth. Phillips writes:

> William Shakespear, the Glory of the English Stage; whose nativity at Stratford upon Avon, is the highest honour that Town can boast of: from an Actor of Tragedies and Comedies, he became a Maker; and such a Maker, that though some others may perhaps pretend to a more exact Decorum and oeconomie, especially in Tragedy, never any express't a more lofty and Tragic heighth; never any represented nature more purely to the life, and where the polishments of Art are most wanting, as probably his Learning was not extraordinary, he pleased with a certain wild and native Elegance.

Finally, then, we have all the elements of a poetics for the first three quarters of the seventeenth century. The true poet is a fluent imitator of nature, recreating life in all its richness and people in all their complexity, piercing the soul of reader and audience with passion and eloquence, ignoring "a more exact decorum" and "polishment." In this chorus of praise for the bard, only Jonson muttered that craft was equally essential, and even he came to believe that Shakespeare got along without it. The type of the true poet was William Shakespeare, and the disorderly richness, passion and eloquence of *Antony and Cleopatra* were the marks of the true poem.

THE CHALLENGE to all of this, the C work, came in 1678 with the performance and publication of John Dryden's *All for Love, or The World Well Lost,* a rival treatment of the story of Antony and Cleopatra, "Written in Imitation of Shakespeare's Stile." The play uses the same events, although with considerable differences. As William G. McCollom has said in *Tragedy* that Sophocles would have begun *Romeo and Juliet* in Capulet's tomb, so Dryden begins *All for Love* after the Battle of Actium, or well after the middle of Shakespeare's play. Pompey, Enobarbus, and all other secondary plots are omitted, Octavius Caesar never appears (although Octavia does, and confronts Cleopatra), and the play ends like Shakespeare's except that the final tributes spoken over the corpses of the lovers come from Egyptians, since none of the Roman conquerors is permitted to be present.

Lord David Cecil, in his Ker Memorial Lecture on *Antony and Cleopatra*, has said:

> The play opens with Antony poised at the top of a slope as it were. After a little uncertainty, he begins to slide down, and then proceeds faster and faster until he reaches the bottom. The play would have been better entitled 'The Decline and Fall of Antony.'

This is much truer of *All for Love*, if it is true of *Antony and Cleopatra* at all. In place of Shakespeare's series of transcendences, Dryden's play has a single action clearly expressed in the title and subtitle: the world well lost for love. Cleopatra is worth more to Antony than the world, and forced to choose, he chooses Cleopatra. Antony states this clearly at the end of the second act:

> Give, you Gods,
> Give to your Boy, your Cesar,
> This Rattle of a Globe to play withal,
> This Gu-gau World, and put him cheaply off:
> I'll not be pleas'd with less than Cleopatra.

The play is enormously tighter than Shakespeare's. Where we see Shakespeare's Octavia betrothed to Antony in Rome and living with him in Athens, Dryden's Octavia appears onstage only when Ventidius summons her to Alexandria, along with Antony's two little daughters. While Shakespeare's Antony is carried dying to the monument where Cleopatra and her attendants are hiding, Dryden's Cleopatra comes with her maids to the Temple of Isis where Antony lives, where all the action transpires, and where Antony now lies dying. The form the action takes is a series of what James Joyce in *Ulysses* calls "French triangles." Where they were implicit in Shakespeare, Dryden has made them explicit. First Ventidius, Antony's loyal general (Dryden's substitute for Enobarbus), tries to win Antony away from Cleopatra, appealing to their comradeship in arms. He disparages Cleopatra strongly, even to the point of muttering such comments on her remarks as "False Crocodyle!" Then young Dollabella, "the bravest youth of Rome," appears to make a triangle with Antony and Octavius. Of Dollabella's friendship with Octavius, Antony says:

> Whom Caesar loves beyond the love of
>   Women;
> He could resolve his mind, as Fire does Wax,
> From that hard rugged Image, melt him down,
> And mould him in what softer form he pleas'd.

Of his own friendship with Dollabella, Antony says:

> He lov'd me too,
> I was his Soul; he liv'd not but in me;
> We were so clos'd within each others breasts,
> The rivets were not found that join'd us first
> That does not reach us yet: we were so mixt,
> As meeting streams, both to our selves were
>   lost;

We were one mass; we could not give or take,
But from the same; for he was I, I he.

Since Octavius Caesar is not around, Dollabella, as soon as he appears in Alexandria, promptly constitutes a new triangle with Antony and Cleopatra. He had originally been forbidden Cleopatra's sight and sent away, Antony says:

Because I fear'd he lov'd her: he confest
He had a warmth, which, for my sake, he stifled;
For 'twere impossible that two, so one,
Should not have lov'd the same.

Ventidius, still hopelessly fighting Cleopatra in *his* triangle, attempts to compromise Cleopatra with Dollabella, "To ruine her yet more with Antony." Cleopatra has at the same time been instructed by her eunuch Alexas to vamp Dollabella (I am afraid "vamp" is the only suitable verb) in order to win back Antony through jealousy. All of these schemes and triangles come together when Dollabella brings Cleopatra Antony's farewell. To advance his own suit, Dollabella turns Antony's loving message into bitter attack, at which Cleopatra faints. Dollabella, stricken, immediately confesses his untruth. Cleopatra confesses that she encouraged him to make Antony jealous, and that she loves only Antony. The scene ends with Dollabella kissing Cleopatra's hand in perfect innocent understanding. That scene, observed by the angles of two other triangles, Ventidius and Octavia, is reported to Antony. Ventidius builds it up:

And then he grew familiar with her hand,
Squeez'd it, and worry'd it with ravenous kisses;
She blush'd, and sigh'd, and smil'd, and blush'd again;
At last she took occasion to talk softly,
And brought her cheek up close, and lean'd on his:
At which, he whisper'd kisses back on hers;
And then she cry'd aloud, That constancy
Should be rewarded.

To which Octavia, lying for *her* purposes, adds: "This I saw and heard."

The final triangle is of course Octavia, Antony, and Cleopatra. When Octavia appears with the children, she apparently wins Antony, who embraces them and blubbers:

I am vanquish'd: take me,
Octavia; take me, Children; share me all.
I've been a thriftless Debtor to your loves,
And run out much, in riot, from your stock;
But all shall be amended.

Octavia then confronts Cleopatra triumphantly, drives her to admit that now in defeat she wants only to die, and sweeps out triumphantly with the line:

Be't so then; take thy wish.

The third act ends with Cleopatra going off to her room to weep. The action of the last two acts consists of Antony's discovery, despite new doubts, that he loves Cleopatra more than anything, and her victory over Ventidius, Octavia, and every other rival. At the end of the play Antony has been torn out of all the triangles to be united with Cleopatra in the perfect circle of death.

The characters have not much in common with Shakespeare's. Antony, stricken by Actium, begins the play as a kind of wild man, telling the audience in soliloquy:

> Stay, I fancy
> I'm now turn'd wild, a Commoner of Nature;
> Of all forsaken, and forsaking all;
> Live in a shady Forrest's Sylvan Scene,
> Stretch'd at my length beneath some blasted Oke;
> I lean my head upon the Mossy Bark,
> And look just of a piece, as I grew from it:
> My uncomb'd Locks, matted like Misleto,
> Hang o're my hoary Face; a murm'ring Brook
> Runs at my foot.

He soon emerges as what T. Campbell in his edition of the plays called "a weak voluptuary." When Cleopatra sends him a ruby bracelet, "set with bleeding hearts," ostensibly in farewell but actually to win him back, Ventidius insists that it be returned, correctly diagnosing it as "poyson'd gifts" (like those Medea sent Creon's daughter). Antony announces his intention to keep it in sensual memory of Cleopatra. He says:

What, to refuse her Bracelet! On my Soul,
When I lye pensive in my Tent alone,
'Twill pass the wakeful hours of Winter nights,
To tell these pretty Beads upon my arm,
To count for every one a soft embrace,
A melting kiss at such and such a time;
And now and then the fury of her love.

When Ventidius then calls him an unwashable Ethiope, Antony says, using the name in a sense very unlike Shakespeare's:

I'm a Roman,
Bred to the rules of soft humanity.

In his first confrontation with Cleopatra, however, Antony shows considerable eloquence and more strength than Campbell credits. He charges:

While within your arms I lay,
The World fell mouldring from my hands each hour,
And left me scarce a grasp (I thank your love for't.)

Later, in his last scene with Octavia, Antony states the essence of his character, the paradox of weakness and strength:

For I can ne'er be conquer'd but by love;
And you do all for duty.

His final self-image, when he has driven Octavia away by showing that he still loves Cleopatra, is of transparency:

> Why was I fram'd with this plain honest heart,
> Which knows not to disguise its griefs and
>   weakness,
> But bears its workings outward to the World?
> I should have kept the mighty anguish in,
> And forc'd a smile at Cleopatra's falshood:
> Octavia had believ'd it, and had staid;
> But I am made a shallow-forded Stream,
> Seen to the bottom: all my clearness scorn'd,
> And all my faults expos'd!

Cleopatra begins as the slave of passion, the love-smitten. When Iras suggests, "Call Reason to assist you," Cleopatra answers:

> I have none.
> And none would have: my Love's a noble
>   madness,
> Which shows the cause deserv'd it. Moderate
>   sorrow
> Fits vulgar Love; and for a vulgar Man:
> But I have lov'd with such transcendent pas-
>   sion,
> I soard, at first, quite out of Reasons view,
> And now am lost above it.

The bleeding hearts on the bracelet are perfectly representative of this lady. In Cleopatra's first scene with Antony, Aristotle would have said that where he speaks like a statesman, she speaks like a rhetorician, in the address beginning:

> How shall I plead my cause, when you, my Judge
> Already have condemn'd me? Shall I bring
> The Love you bore me for my Advocate?

Octavia describes her to Antony as "an abandon'd, faithless Prostitute," but Cleopatra's self-image is of a good girl somehow gone wrong, with the same sense of transparency Antony has. When Alexas asks her to vamp Dollabella, Cleopatra replies:

> Can I do this? Ah no; my love's so true,
> That I can neither hide it where it is,
> Nor show it where it is not. Nature meant me
> A Wife, a silly harmless household Dove,
> Fond without art; and kind without deceit;
> But Fortune, that has made a Mistress of me,
> Has thrust me out to the wide World, unfurnish'd
> Of falshood to be happy.

After she confesses her innocent feigning to Dollabella, he pays her a rather beautiful tribute in those terms, saying:

> I find your breast fenc'd round from humane reach,
> Transparent as a Rock of solid Crystal;
> Seen through, but never pierc'd.

Of the minor characters, the most interesting is the eunuch Alexas. Early in the play, he does Cleopatra's thinking and plotting for her, and she obeys him. He is given to the stage asides of a comic villain. When his plot appears to be successful and Cleopatra is winning Antony back, Alexas mutters: "He melts; We conquer." He emerges as fully human only in his soliloquy in Act Three against the eunuch state, concluding:

> She dies for love, but she has known its joys:
> Gods, is this just, that I, who know no joys,
> Must die, because she loves?

Alexas' last scene in the fifth act begins when Antony and Ventidius catch him unprepared, and Alexas cries out to the audience: "My gift of lying's gone." It soon returns, however, and his final desperate lie, that Cleopatra has killed herself with a dagger, brings on the real deaths of Antony and Cleopatra.

The other interesting minor character is Octavia, who is imaged as an odd combination of stern Roman duty, nobly motivated by "a Wife's Virtue," and the sort of whining self-pitier we know best from soap opera. When Octavia sends the children across the stage to win back Antony, she says:

> Go, I say, and pull him to me,
> And pull him to your selves, from that bad
> Woman.

You, Agrippina, hang upon his arms;
And you, Antonia, clasp about his waste:
If he will shake you off, if he will dash you
Against the Pavement, you must bear it, Children;
For you are mine, and I was born to suffer.

Her other big scene, the confrontation of Cleopatra, was clearly written as a set piece for Mrs. Boutell and Mrs. Corey, the actresses who created it at the Theatre Royal, and has little to do with character. Octavia begins it in words like those of Stanley greeting Livingstone:

I need not ask if you are Cleopatra.

Mrs. Jameson's comment in *Characteristics of Women* seems not unfair:

Dryden has committed a great mistake in bringing Octavia and her children on the scene, and in immediate contact with Cleopatra. To have thus violated the truth of history might have been excusable, but to sacrifice the truth of nature and dramatic propriety, to produce a mere stage effect, was unpardonable. In order to preserve the unity of interest, he has falsified the character of Octavia as well as that of Cleopatra: he has presented us with a regular scolding match between the rivals, in which they come sweeping up to each other from opposite

> sides of the stage, with their respective trains,
> like two pea-hens in a passion.

Dryden's language and metaphor, impressive enough in isolation, suffer inevitably in comparison with Shakespeare's. The play has many Shakespearian echoes: Alexas' "But, since our will/Is lamely follow'd by our pow'r" echoes Enobarbus; Antony smashes the cosmos rhetorically like his prototype, "Sink the props of Heav'n,/And fall the Skyes to crush the neather World"; Antony describes Cleopatra's barge like Enobarbus (Plutarch being the common source) with the odd switch that at the end of the speech it is not Cleopatra who pants breathlessly but the watching crowd; Cleopatra goes tragically to her chamber in words resembling Shakespeare's, "Lead me, my Charmian; nay, your hand too, Iras"; Enobarbus' tribute "The holy priests/Bless her when she is riggish" becomes Ventidius' "The holy Priests gaze on her when she smiles"; the words of Caesar's beautiful tribute, "grace" and "toils," are picked up out of context; the last words of Dryden's Charmian are:

> Yes, 'tis well done, and like a Queen, the last
> Of her great Race: I follow her.

Dryden's language is most successful when he is furthest from Shakespeare. At his best, his lines have a vigorous blank-verse rhythm, rocked by a strong caesura, owing nothing to his illustrious predecessor:

Sea-Horses floundring in the slimy mud,
Toss'd up their heads, and dash'd the ooze
about 'em.

His metaphors are happiest when entirely original, like Antony's comparison of himself to the grape harvest:

In the full Vintage of my flowing honors,
Sate still, and saw it prest by other hands.
Fortune came smiling to my youth, and woo'd
it
And purple greatness met my ripen'd years.

If some of Dryden's ideas are worse than unfortunate, like having Octavia call Cleopatra "that bad Woman," he can sometimes take a poor idea, such as having Cleopatra crown the head of dead Antony with laurel, and redeem it with language whose moving, sparse eloquence owes little to Shakespeare. Answering Charmian's "What must be done?" as they prepare for death, Cleopatra says:

Short Ceremony, Friends;
But yet it must be decent. First, this Laurel
Shall crown my Hero's head: he fell not basely,
Nor left his Shield behind him. Only thou
Cou'dst triumph o'er thy self; and thou alone
Wert worthy so to triumph.

Dryden was delighted with *All for Love*, which he said was the only play he wrote to please himself, and so was the audience, if we may judge by the fact that for a century it drove *Antony and Cleopatra* off the stage, and up to a hundred years ago had been performed ten times as often.

THE SANCTION for *All for Love*, the powerful critical statement that accommodates to the work challenging an earlier standard and legitimizes it, was written by John Dryden himself. It is the preface to the play, "Antony and Cleopatra and the Art of Tragedy," published with it in 1678. This is the first example we shall meet of the poet as his own critical sanctioner, and Dryden is one of the tiny group of first-rate English poets who were also first-rate critics. He says in the preface, with his usual moderation and good sense:

> Poets themselves are the most proper, though I conclude not the only critics.

Dryden's preface discusses not only his own play but Shakespeare's and its author, as well as many general problems of tragedy, poetry, and criticism.

As a pioneer of the English neo-classic revolution, Dryden fittingly takes many moderate positions in the preface, compromising the rigidities of continental neo-classicism to the English Shakespearian tradition, as eighteenth-century critics, secure in the later assurances of the Augustan age, would not. Having done so much to make his play conform to the unities that critics like Castelvetro had developed from Aristotle's single Unity of Action, Dryden writes honestly:

> The fabric of the play is regular enough, as to the inferior parts of it; and the Unities of Time, Place, and Action, more exactly observed than perhaps the English theatre requires.

Sir Walter Scott, in his introduction to *All for Love*, argued much more strongly than the author that the unities had been successful in giving Dryden "the advantage to be derived from a simplicity and concentration of plot," and that "the plan of Dryden's play must be unequivocally preferred to that of Shakespeare in point of coherence, unity, and simplicity."

In his preface, Dryden also takes a middle position between what he believes to be Shakespeare's bawdy natural license and later prudishness. He writes:

> 'Tis true, some actions, though natural, are not fit to be represented; and broad obscenities in words ought in good manners to be avoided; expressions therefore are a modest clothing of our thoughts, as breeches and petticoats are of our bodies. If I have kept myself within the bounds of modesty, all beyond it is but nicety and affectation; which is no more but modesty depraved into a vice.

His comment on the French drama of Racine and Corneille, as opposed to that of Shakespeare, is similarly equivocal:

> Yet in this nicety of manners does the excellency of French poetry consist: their heroes are the most civil people breathing; but their good breeding seldom extends to a word of sense; all their wit is in their ceremony; they want the genius which animates our stage; and therefore 'tis but necessary, when they cannot please, that they should take care not to offend. But as the civilest man in the company is commonly the dullest, so these authors, while they are afraid to make you laugh or cry, out of pure good manners make you sleep.

Dryden states his preference for the *Hippolytus* of Euripides over the *Phèdre* of Racine, but even with his beloved Greeks, Dryden will not go all the way. "I have endeavoured in this play to follow the practice of the Ancients," he says, then adds:

> Yet, though their models are regular, they are too little for English tragedy; which requires to be built in a larger compass. I could give an instance in the *Oedipus Tyrannus*, which was the masterpiece of Sophocles; but I reserve it for a more fit occasion, which I hope to have hereafter.

His conclusion is boldly "I desire to be tried by the laws of my own country."

Dryden's preface accepts Aristotle as the standard of criticism so completely that without mentioning him by name he says:

> All reasonable men have long since concluded, that the hero of the poem ought not to be a character of perfect virtue, for then he could not, without injustice, be made unhappy; nor yet altogether wicked, because he could not then be pitied.

He accepts that pity, if not fear, is the aim of tragedy, and complains of the plot he took from Shakespeare:

> That which is wanting to work up the pity to a greater height, was not afforded me by the story; for the crimes of love, which they both committed, were not occasioned by any necessity, or fatal ignorance, but were wholly voluntary; since our passions are, or ought to be, within our power.

Dryden admits that his Octavia was a mistake, but not for our reasons. He writes:

> The greatest error in the contrivance seems to be in the person of Octavia; for, though I might use the privilege of a poet to introduce her into Alexandria, yet I had not enough considered, that the compassion she moved to herself and children was destructive to that which I reserved for Antony and Cleopatra; whose mu-

> tual love being founded upon vice must lessen the favour of the audience to them, when virtue and innocence were oppressed by it.

"The dividing of pity," he adds, "like the cutting of a river into many channels, abated the strength of the natural stream." As a proper Aristotelian, Dryden says that he chose the story for "the excellency of the moral":

> for the chief persons represented were famous patterns of unlawful love; and their end accordingly was unfortunate.

If the effect is didactic, the aim is nevertheless Aristotle's pleasure or delight. Dryden adds the reservation:

> Poetry, which is a picture of Nature, must generally please; but 'tis not to be understood that all parts of it must please every man.

If this equivocal peace is made with Aristotle, ungrudging obeisance is paid to Shakespeare and *Antony and Cleopatra.* Dryden writes:

> In my style, I have professed to imitate the divine Shakespeare; which that I might perform more freely, I have disencumbered myself from rhyme. Not that I condemn my former way, but that this is more proper to my present purpose. I hope I need not to explain myself, that I have not copied my author servilely;

> words and phrases must of necessity receive a change in succeeding ages; but it is almost a miracle that much of his language remains so pure; and that he who began Dramatic Poetry amongst us, untaught by any, and as Ben Jonson tells us, without learning, should by the force of his own genius perform so much, that in a manner he has left no praise for any who come after him.

He concludes:

> Yet, I hope I may affirm, and without vanity, that, by imitating him, I have excelled myself throughout the play.

However, just as Dryden's preface bows to Shakespeare, it also bows to Thomas Rymer, Dryden's contemporary and Shakespeare's most vicious neo-classic critic. It was Rymer who called *Othello* the "Tragedy of the Handkerchief," said that its moral was that wives should look well to their linen, and dismissed it as "a Bloody Farce, without salt or savour." "Mr. Rymer has judiciously observed," Dryden says, that the ancients "are and ought to be our masters." In short, Dryden's preface states a moderate case for the right of his own tight play to exist as well as Shakespeare's vasty one, but he introduces all the neo-classic criteria that will justify the literature of the next age. The ground is laid for Samuel Johnson, who eventually found the action of *Antony and Cleopatra* to be "produced without any art of connection or care of disposition," and for a century that took as its keynote for poetry Dryden's view that "our passions are, or ought to be, within our power."

III

English Romanticism

THE STANDARD poem of the eighteenth century might be considered to be Alexander Pope's "The Rape of the Lock," published in 1712 and republished in a considerably revised version in 1714. The occasion for the poem was a tiny scandal. Lord Petre had cut off a lock of Miss Arabella Fermor's hair and refused to return it, and the incident had caused bad feeling between the two families. Pope's friend John Caryll, who was friendly with both families, Pope told Joseph Spence, "desired me to write a poem to make a jest of it, and laugh them together again." Pope produced a poem of two cantos in iambic pentameter couplets within a fortnight, and it appears to have had the desired effect. Despite Addison's advice that the poem was "a delicious little thing" as it stood and not to tamper with it, Pope felt that it could be made more ambitious, and in 1714 he expanded it to five cantos, with additional scenes and an elaborate mock-epic machinery of Rosicrucian supernaturals that he got from a book called the *Comte de Gabalis*. In its final version, "The Rape of the Lock" first describes the elaborate toilet of Belinda, tended by her guardian sylph, Ariel, and other supernaturals. She and another maiden, Clarissa, then have an epic combat at ombre with the baron and another gentleman, at which the baron cuts off one of Belinda's tresses. The gnome Umbriel journeys to the underworld Cave of Spleen to return with a load of wild female emotions, and there is a furious Homeric battle between men and women, in the course of which the lock disappears, to reappear in the sky as a comet with a hairy tail, writing Belinda's name immortal.

The principal effect the poem gives at every point is of order and control. Its action, described in resounding epic imagery, is always tiny. The baron's madness comes from the mildest of intoxicants:

> Coffee (which makes the politician wise,
> And see through all things with his half-shut eyes)
> Sent up in vapours to the baron's brain
> New stratagems, the radiant lock to gain.

Belinda's reaction when the lock is cut off, which we can assume to be wounded vanity, is put in heroic terms, then ironically undercut:

> Then flash'd the living lightning from her eyes,
> And screams of horror rend th'affrighted skies.
> Not louder shrieks to pitying Heaven are cast,

When husbands, or when lapdogs breathe their
last.

Passions, as Dryden advised, are carefully kept under control. Instead of Cleopatra's soul-consuming love, we are told of such virgins as Belinda:

With varying vanities, from every part,
They shift the moving toyshop of their heart.

In the last canto, in a speech Pope added in 1717, Clarissa appeals to two of the highest virtues of the Augustan age. She says:

How vain are all these glories, all our pains,
Unless good sense preserve what beauty gains.

and adds:

What then remains, but well our power to use,
And keep good humour still, whate'er we lose?

The "good sense" and "good humour" Clarissa summons up are the poet's virtues too. Pope told Spence of the critic William Walsh:

He used to encourage me much, and used to tell me, that there was one way left of excelling; for though we had several great poets, we never had any one great poet that was correct; and desired me to make that my study and aim.

Like its subject, the poem too is a game within clearly defined rules. We can imagine Pope writing his hundreds of couplets, with hardly a feminine rhyme in the entire poem, as a *tour de force* not unlike the baron's, and encompassing a whole range of feeling within the confines of the stylized like Belinda playing at ombre.

If we are tempted to read more into the poem than its trivialities, we had our warning early. In 1715, a year after the complete "Rape of the Lock" was published, one Esdras Barnivelt published a pamphlet: *A Key to the Lock, or a Treatise proving beyond all contradiction the dangerous tendency of a late Poem, intitled the Rape of the Lock, to Religion and Government.* In it Barnivelt showed that Belinda represents Great Britain, that the lock is the barrier treaty and the baron who cuts it off the Earl of Oxford, that Clarissa is Lady Masham, Sir Plume Prince Eugene, and so on. "Esdras Barnivelt" was of course Alexander Pope, having some fun with the tendency of his time to find hidden political meanings, and not averse to stirring up a little controversy about his poem. The tendency of our time has been to find other kinds of hidden meanings. It would be equally ludicrous to produce a Freudian interpretation in which the poem is a projection of Pope's castration complex, or Belinda is ego, the baron id, and Clarissa superego; or a Marxian interpretation with Belinda the English yeomanry expropriated by baronial enclosures and forcibly proletarianized; or a Frazerian interpretation in which Belinda is the corn maiden reaped by the annual baron in a fertility ritual. The solar mythologists of the nineteenth century would have shown, with plenty of apt quotations from the poem, that Belinda is the sun, descending at night into the Cave of Spleen and rising in splendor in the heavens the next morning. Esdras Barnivelt might have written any of these.

Nevertheless, the poem is clearly much more meaningful than its surface. We cannot accept it, as the nineteenth century did, as the "bit of filigree-work" William Hazlitt calls it, or as Leslie Stephen's "brilliant, sparkling, vivacious trifle." There is a sense in which Pope is a very knowing Freudian. The poem is one vast comic symbolic defloration, proper to a cruelly deformed poet for whom such ventures were symbolic or nothing. The hair is a fertility or sex symbol, described in the poem as catching men as it traps birds and hooks fish. "Lock" is a pun on Freud's lock that all keys fit, and it is a pun that Pope makes explicit in the title of his Barnivelt pamphlet. Its rape by the baron is a sex act, and the baron cries triumphantly to Belinda at the end of Canto Four:

> What wonder then, fair nymph! thy hairs should feel
> The conquering force of unresisted steel?

Its loss is the unalterable loss of virginity, comically contrasted with "a wretched sylph" who gets in the way of the shears and is cut in half, then is given Pope's parenthetical reassurance "(But airy substance soon unites again)" that he is unlike flesh-

and-blood substance. We get the same comedy in the free-for-all, with Belinda's impossible demand:

> "Restore the lock!" she cries; and all around
> "Restore the lock!" the vaulted roofs rebound.

If the card game is a stylized seduction (when the Queen of Hearts is taken, "the blood the virgin's cheek forsook"), Belinda's punishment of the baron, the pinch of snuff that makes him sneeze and sneeze, is parody orgasm. In this world that Freud and Pope share,

> Men prove with child, as powerful fancy
> works,
> And maids, turn'd bottles, call aloud for corks.

Belinda's remark to the baron,

> O hadst thou, cruel! been content to seize
> Hairs less in sight, or any hairs but these!

may be her conscious pubic-hair joke (Cleanth Brooks, in *The Well Wrought Urn*, thinks it is not) but it is certainly Pope's. The battle in the last canto is a torrent of double meaning. Pope writes:

> Now Jove suspends his golden scales in air,
> Weighs the men's wits against the lady's hair;
> The doubtful beam long nods from side to side;
> At length the wits mount up, the hairs subside.

The baron, "Who sought no more than on his foe to die," warns Belinda when she has him helplessly sneezing, "Thou by some other shalt be laid as low." Brooks has noted the frail china jars that symbolize virginity in the poem: broken as an alternative to breaking "Diana's law" in Canto Two, fallen into fragments when the lock is cut off in Canto Three, recollected as having been tottering that morning in Canto Four.

Without reading Marx, Pope is just as clear about social context in the poem. He carefully shows us the glittering falsity of leisure class life, with much of the gold really gilt: "gilded chariots," "gilded mast," novels "neatly gilt." While Belinda dresses in the third canto, the real world of social institutions, production and exchange goes on:

> The hungry judges soon the sentence sign,
> And wretches hang that jurymen may dine;
> The merchant from th' Exchange returns in peace,
> And the long labours of the toilet cease.

It is this dichotomy of two worlds or classes that underlies the poem's principal stylistic device, the comic yoking of two objects of very different degrees of importance with one verb, a rhetorical device called "zeugma." Thus:

> Or stain her honour, or her new brocade;

> Here Britain's statesmen oft the fall foredoom
> Of foreign tyrants, and of nymphs at home;
> Here thou, great Anna! whom three realms obey,

> Dost sometimes counsel take—and sometimes
> tea.

While the lesser world of events—brocades, nymphs, and tea or tay—go on in the poem, the significant events of the social, political, and economic world are clearly visible through its gossamer texture.

Pope certainly knew as much as Frazer and the Cambridge scholars about ritual. Superficially, "The Rape of the Lock" is a parody of religion, and it is interesting to know that both the families involved were Roman Catholic, as was Pope. Belinda's toilet is called a "holy ritual" and is actually, as G. Wilson Knight has pointed out in *The Burning Oracle*, a ritual in the Eros cult, in which Belinda is both priestess and goddess, a priestess in her own worship. The divine tress is naturally "sacred." We see the baron at his worship:

> For this, ere Phoebus rose, he had implor'd
> Propitious Heaven, and every power ador'd,
> But chiefly Love—to Love an altar built,
> Of twelve vast French romances, neatly gilt.
> There lay three garters, half a pair of gloves,
> And all the trophies of his former loves;
> With tender billet-doux he lights the pyre,
> And breathes three amorous sighs to raise the
> fire.

The coffee-making and drinking are described as a sacred ceremonial in Canto Three, and like many such, quickly turn orgiastic.

Deeper than these parodies of religious ritual are the poem's two epic battles, the mock-warfare of the card game and the free-for-all between the beaux and belles at the end, both rigidly stylized and ceremonial. Cards, love, and war are equated as games with identical rules, and sex and mock-death are ambivalent consummations that turn into each other. In the second canto, Belinda arms herself for the fray like a Homeric warrior, putting on a sevenfold petticoat like the shield of Achilles: "stiff with hoops, and arm'd with ribs of whale." She is a mock-combatant in a ritual battle, who must lose and be symbolically slain to win and be reborn. Deeper still, the poem is the great myth or the great journey of ritual, the descent into the belly of the whale or the Cave of Spleen:

> Now glaring fiends, and snakes on rolling spires,
> Pale spectres, gaping tombs, and purple fires.

followed by emergence transformed. Belinda starts in *hubris* and is chastened, starts in Edenic innocence and has a Fall, becomes another "maid" "to numerous ills betray'd." Then Clarissa as initiator can reveal the mystery to her. Like the Orphic "A kid, I have fallen into milk," this is that in time "locks will turn to gray," but that this one lock, like her immortal soul, can be taken out of time. It will be eternal, perpetually fair, in a comet or a constellation, in heaven, in a poem by Alexander Pope. Initiate maidens in primitive cultures are ritually deflowered, scarified, circumcized, have their teeth filed or knocked out; Belinda loses a lock of hair and becomes a woman.

I have thus done precisely what I said I would not and should not do, found vast significances in Pope's poem, written in high spirits in his early twenties, "intended only to divert a few young ladies." The Rosicrucian machinery of air sylphs, earth gnomes, fire salamanders and water nymphs points at Pope's division of women into four comparable types; coquettes, prudes, termagants and acquiescents. But Belinda, a nymph, or docile, aspires to be a sylph or coquette and soon transcends everything by becoming a goddess; Clarissa, identified as a prude, emerges as a true wisdom figure. Here as elsewhere the poem demolishes its own machinery, as though it too aspired to break through the polished surface into significance. When Walsh advised Pope to become the first "correct" poet, he meant, in Austin Warren's paraphrase in *Rage for Order*, "The age of myth-making is over." However, just as a mock-epic is not a mockery of the epic but a kind of epic in symbolic and ironic terms, so it requires a mock-myth equally valid although symbolic and ironic.

A poem that deliberately invites comparison, by specific reference, to Homer and the Bible, Dante and Shakespeare, Spenser and Milton, is less apt to be setting out to parody the whole of our literary culture than attempting to build on it ironically. A good part of the nineteenth century saw Pope's poetry as "spoonfulls of boiling oil, ladled out by a fiendish monkey at an upstairs window." The twentieth century, represented by John Middleton Murry, F. R. Leavis, and Brooks, has tended to see Pope as a serious metaphysical poet like Donne. He need not be either, really. Brooks reminds us that a few years after Pope published "The Rape of the Lock," his good friend Jonathan Swift wrote "The Lady's Dressing Room," in which the toilet of a society belle like Belinda is seen as infinitely foul and evil. Pope sees everything that Swift sees, but he nevertheless regards the event as comic, absurd, rather touching, somewhat beautiful. Belinda making up, like Pope, is an artist reordering nature. Pope must affirm the incident of the rape of the lock as important to show its ultimate triviality, must mock it in terms of epic and myth to show its considerable significance. He must see whole heavens and earths in a lock of hair to tell us something serious and important about the small spot we live in. Pope's vision of girls like Belinda shifting "the moving toyshop of their heart" is uniquely his own, but it is not so terribly far from Yeats' ultimate vision, the place where all the ladders start, "the foul rag-and-bone shop of the heart."

THE POETICS for "The Rape of the Lock" is Samuel Johnson's "Alexander Pope" in *Lives of the English Poets,* published in 1780. It includes not only a full biography, but what used to be called a "character," a detailed criticism of the works, a comparison of Dryden and Pope, and an appended review of Pope's epitaphs. Johnson's criteria for poetry are perhaps clearer in "Alexander Pope" than anywhere else.

"Nature" shifts in meaning from the seventeenth century, as it will shift again in the nineteenth. Johnson makes it clear that physical nature, the country, is not the fittest material for poetry. Of the "Epistle from Eloisa to Abelard," he writes:

> The gloom of a convent strikes the imagination with far greater force than the solitude of a grove.

There is another sense of the word, however. Homer's representations are "natural," an "open display of unadulterated nature." Johnson sounds rather like a premature Emersonian when he writes of Pope:

> He gathered his notions fresh from reality, not from the copies of authors, but the originals of Nature.

What Johnson means, of course, is human nature, not landscape. We can see how radically the word changes its meanings when we see Thomas De Quincey in the next century taking precisely the opposite view, that Pope paid no attention to nature. De Quincey writes in his essay on Wordsworth:

> Pope, again, and many who live in towns, make such blunders as that of supposing the moon to tip with silver the hills *behind* which she is rising, not by erroneous use of their eyes (for they use them not at all), but by inveterate preconceptions.

De Quincey clearly means landscape.

Johnson's "nature" and "natural" imply fitness, even decorum; thus blank verse is alien to "the nature of our language." One of the "natural" qualities of a poet is ingenuity or fancy. Johnson praises "The Rape of the Lock" as "the most airy, the most ingenious, and the most delightful" of all Pope's compositions. Mental energy seems to be the chief ingredient of what Johnson defines as poetic "genius." He writes:

> Pope had likewise genius; a mind active, ambitious, and adventurous, always investigating, always aspiring; in its widest searches still longing to go forward, in its highest flights still wishing to be higher; always imagining something greater than it knows, always endeavouring more than it can do.

In his comparison of Pope and Dryden, Johnson defines the quality more clearly:

> Of genius, that power which constitutes a poet; that quality without which judgment is cold, and knowledge is inert; that energy which collects, combines, amplifies, and animates; the

> superiority must, with some hesitation, be allowed to Dryden.

Later Johnson writes:

> Pope had, in proportions very nicely adjusted to each other, all the qualities that constitute genius.

He goes on to define them as "Invention," instancing "The Rape of the Lock," "Imagination," and "Judgment." With the Gothic aspect of Pope's imagination, however, Johnson has little sympathy. Discussing Pope's grotto at Twickenham, decorated with fossil bodies, Johnson dismisses it with one of his smashing antitheses: "And vanity produced a grotto where necessity enforced a passage."

Opposed to all the qualities in poetry generally and Pope specifically that can be subsumed under "nature" are those that can be classified under "order." Poetic order is imposed by artifice, Johnson says, but it then appears natural. He writes:

> Almost every poem consisting of precepts is so far arbitrary and immethodical, that many of the paragraphs may change places with no apparent inconvenience; for of two or more positions, depending upon some remote and general principle, there is seldom any cogent reason why one should precede the other. But for the order in which they stand, whatever it be, a little ingenuity may easily give a reason. 'It is possible,' says Hooker, 'that, by long cir-

> cumduction from any one truth, all truths may be inferred.' Of all homogeneous truths, at least of all truths respecting the same general end, in whatever series they may be produced, a concatenation by intermediate ideas may be formed, such as, when it is once shown, shall appear natural; but if this order be reversed, another mode of connection equally specious may be found or made.

Characteristically, the essential constituent of metrical compositions is defined as "the stated recurrence of settled numbers." The emphasis is on reason, order, and artifice, and the principal poetic quality they will produce is elegance; not the "wild and native elegance" for which Phillips praised Shakespeare, but something more decorous. "Pope cannot be denied to excel his masters in variety and elegance," Johnson writes. He generalizes:

> Thus it will be found, in the progress of learning, that in all nations the first writers are simple, and that every age improves in elegance.

Ontogeny recapitulates phylogeny in the process of each poet's rewriting, and Johnson describes the progress of the poet's mind "from the rudeness of its first conceptions to the elegance of its last."

Johnson's emphasis is thus strongly on rewriting, and his highest praise for Pope is as a tireless reviser. He remarks that despite Addison's advice about leaving "The Rape of the Lock" alone, Pope commendably "saw that it was capable of improvement" and did something about it. He "was never content with mediocrity when excellence could be attained," Johnson writes, continuing:

> He considered poetry as the business of his life; and, however he might seem to lament his occupation, he followed it with constancy; to make verses was his first labour, and to mend them was his last.

Johnson adds:

> The method of Pope, as may be collected from his translation, was to write his first thoughts in his first words, and gradually to amplify, decorate, rectify, and refine them.

Ultimately, Pope's rewriting becomes a moral attribute or an act of virtue:

> Pope was not content to satisfy; he desired to excel, and therefore always endeavoured to do his best; he did not court the candour, but dared the judgment of his reader, and, expecting no indulgence from others, he showed none to himself. He examined lines and words with minute and punctilious observation, and retouched every part with indefatigable diligence, till he had nothing left to be forgiven.

"What is easy is seldom excellent," Johnson concludes.

The primary aim of Pope's rewriting was smoothness. Johnson talks of "the smoothness of his numbers," or his rewriting of Donne's *Satires* "in smoother numbers," and of the quality he learned from Dryden as "the rejection of unnatural thoughts and rugged numbers." Praising "Eloisa to Abelard," Johnson says: "Here is no crudeness of sense, nor asperity of language." The secondary aim was clarity, or the avoidance of "obscurity." "It will seldom be found that he altered," Johnson writes, "without adding clearness, elegance, or vigour." Johnson sums it all up:

> Of his intellectual character, the constituent and fundamental principle was good sense, a prompt and intuitive perception of consonance and propriety.

Johnson recognizes the limits of that virtue, however. He continues:

> But good sense alone is a sedate and quiescent quality, which manages its possessions well, but does not increase them; it collects few materials for its own operations, and preserves safety, but never gains supremacy.

Good sense would have accomplished nothing, Johnson goes on to say, without Pope's genius. At the same time, Johnson feels that some bolder quality is lacking, as his comparison with Dryden makes clear. Some of Johnson's tributes seem oddly ambivalent, as when he writes:

> With such faculties, and such dispositions, he excelled every other writer in poetical pru-

dence; he wrote in such a manner as might expose him to few hazards.

With all his emphasis on genius ordered by good sense, and elegance attained by painstaking mending, it is no wonder that Johnson found "The Rape of the Lock" so airy, ingenious and delightful. In his estimate of the works, he begins:

> To the praises which have been accumulated on *The Rape of the Lock* by readers of every class, from the critic to the waiting-maid, it is difficult to make any addition. Of that which is universally allowed to be the most attractive of all ludicrous compositions, let it rather be now inquired from what sources the power of pleasing is derived.

Johnson sees the poem's supernaturals as a perfect example of decorum: "they give their proper help, and do their proper mischief." He adds:

> In this work are exhibited, in a very high degree, the two most engaging powers of an author. New things are made familiar, and familiar things are made new.

His conclusion is that the poem may have slight faults, "but what are such faults to so much excellence?"

Pope's nastiest critic, John Dennis, who distinguished himself by writing that Pope's muse was poxed and that he himself was a "short, squab gentleman," waited fourteen years after the poem was printed to publish an attack. In it he said, among other things, that the poem lacked a moral, and he contrasted it unfavorably with a now-forgotten poem by Boileau that exposed the pride and discord of the clergy. Powerfully reinforced by his prejudices, Johnson answers Dennis:

> Perhaps neither Pope nor Boileau has made the world much better than he found it; but, if they had both succeeded, it were easy to tell who would have deserved most from public gratitude. The freaks, and humours, and spleen, and vanity of women, as they embroil families in discord, and fill houses with disquiet, do more to obstruct the happiness of life in a year than the ambition of the clergy in many centuries.

"The Rape of the Lock" may ultimately be no more for Johnson than an engaging satire on women, but his critical emphasis creates a world of taste in which its special combination of good sense and good humor can be swept up to the heavens, like poor Belinda's tress.

AN adequate CHALLENGE to this world of artifice and decorum comes with a poem published early in the next century. It is "Resolution and Independence," by William Wordsworth, written in

1802 and published five years later. Originally called "The Leech Gatherer," it tells of the poet's inspiring encounter with an old leech gatherer when the poet was in a mood of bleak depression. It is written in twenty rime royal stanzas, iambic pentameter with a rhyme-scheme of ABABBCC.

We know of the incident on which the poem is based from an entry in the Grasmere journal of Wordsworth's sister Dorothy, under the date of October 3, 1800. She writes:

> N. B. When Wm. and I returned from accompanying Jones, we met an old man almost double. He had on a coat, thrown over his shoulders, above his waistcoat and coat. Under this he carried a bundle, and had an apron and a nightcap. His face was interesting. He had dark eyes and a long nose. John, who afterwards met him at Wytheburn, took him for a Jew. He was of Scotch parents, but had been born in the army. He had had a wife, and 'a good woman, and it pleased God to bless us with ten children.' All these were dead but one, of whom he had not heard for many years, a sailor. His trade was to gather leeches, but now leeches are scarce, and he had not strength for it. He lived by begging, and was making his way to Carlisle, where he should buy a few godly books to sell. He said leeches were very scarce, partly owing to this dry season, but many years they have been scarce—he sup-

posed it owing to their being much sought after, that they did not breed fast, and were of slow growth. Leeches were formerly 2s. 6d. [per] 100; they are now 30s. He had been hurt in driving a cart, his leg broke, his body driven over, his skull fractured. He felt no pain till he recovered from his first insensibility. It was then late in the evening, when the light was just going away.

In May, 1802, Wordsworth began the poem. Dorothy Wordsworth writes, under May 4:

> I wrote [out] *The Leech Gatherer* for him, which he had begun the night before, and of which he wrote several stanzas in bed this morning. It was very hot; we called at Mr. Simpson's door as we passed, but did not go in. We rested several times by the way, read, and repeated *The Leech Gatherer*.

Three days later she writes:

> William had slept uncommonly well, so, feeling himself strong, he fell to work at *The Leech Gatherer*; he wrote hard at it till dinner time, then he gave over, tired to death—he had finished the poem.

On May 9, Dorothy Wordsworth notes the start of the rewriting:

> William worked at *The Leech Gatherer* almost incessantly from morning till tea-time.

On July 4, two months after he had started the poem and almost two years after the experience, Wordsworth finally concluded his difficult labor, and Dorothy's journal notes "Wm. finished *The Leech Gatherer* today."

The revised "Resolution and Independence" has three stages of action. The first, in the first three stanzas, is a movement from antecedent melancholy to joy, in reaction to nature's innocence and beauty after a storm:

> There was a roaring in the wind all night;
> The rain came heavily and fell in floods;
> But now the sun is rising calm and bright;
> The birds are singing in the distant woods.

He continues:

> All things that love the sun are out of doors;
> The sky rejoices in the morning's birth;
> The grass is bright with rain-drops;—on the moors
> The hare is running races in her mirth;
> And with her feet she from the plashy earth
> Raises a mist; that, glittering in the sun,
> Runs with her all the way, wherever she doth run.

The poet, "a Traveller then upon the moor," sees the hare, hears the birds, and feels "as happy as a boy":

My old remembrances went from me wholly;
And all the ways of men, so vain and melancholy.

As the poet will later say to the old man, "This morning gives us promise of a glorious day."

However, the reassurances of natural beauty and innocence prove inadequate, and the poet is immediately plunged into a deep and apparently unmotivated depression, the poem's second action covering the next four stanzas. Wordsworth writes:

But, as it sometimes chanceth, from the might
Of joy in minds that can no further go,
As high as we have mounted in delight
In our dejection do we sink as low:
To me that morning did it happen so;
And fears and fancies thick upon me came;
Dim sadness—and blind thoughts, I knew not, nor could name.

The poet thinks of what might come upon him:

Solitude, pain of heart, distress, and poverty.

He realizes that he has been careless, improvident for the future, and realizes that he can expect no one to care for him. Then the poet thinks of Chatterton, "the marvellous Boy," dead by his own hand before he was eighteen, and of Burns, "who walked in glory and joy," dying in poverty and misery. The poet concludes:

> We Poets in our youth begin in gladness;
> But thereof come in the end despondency and
> madness.

The poem's third movement begins in the eighth stanza and continues to the end. It consists of a mystic reassurance furnished by the encounter with the leech gatherer. Wordsworth writes:

> Yet it befell that, in this lonely place,
> When I with these untoward thoughts had
> striven,
> Beside a pool bare to the eye of heaven
> I saw a Man before me unawares:
> The oldest man he seemed that ever wore grey
> hairs.

He feels that the old man has been "from some far region sent,"

> To give me human strength, by apt admonish-
> ment.

The poet marvels to find "In that decrepit man so firm a mind," and concludes that in future fits of doubt and dejection,

> I'll think of the Leech-gatherer on the lonely
> moor!

In the popular opinion, which Wordsworth shared, "Resolution and Independence" is a didactic poem. As Wordsworth was reassured by the old leech gatherer, so the reader with similar problems of worry and depression is taught by his example. In

1833, Wordsworth wrote to a friend: "I wish to be considered as a teacher or as nothing." Earlier, in 1807, the year he published "Resolution and Independence," he wrote to Lady Beaumont of his poems:

> Trouble not yourself upon their present reception; of what moment is that compared with what I trust in their destiny?—to console the afflicted; to add sunshine to daylight by making the happy happier; to teach the young and the gracious of every age to see, to think, and feel, and therefore to become more actively and securely virtuous; this is their office.

That seems to me too simple a view. In *Oxford Lectures on Poetry*, A. C. Bradley more shrewdly recognizes that a visionary or apocalyptic quality is the essence of Wordsworth's poetry, and that without it

> *Resolution and Independence* would lose the imaginative atmosphere which adds mystery and grandeur to the apparently simple 'moral.'

This quality is actually the sharp dramatic flash of a transformation, what Kenneth Burke calls a "symbolic action." In "Literature as Equipment for Living" in *The Philosophy of Literary Form*, Burke treats proverbs as symbolic strategies for dealing with human situations, concluding with an extension of his "sociological" categories to all art. Burke writes:

> What would such sociological categories be like? They would consider works of art, I think, as strategies for selecting enemies and allies, for socializing losses, for warding off evil eye, for purification, propitiation, and desanctification, consolation and vengeance, admonition and exhortation, implicit commands or instructions of one sort or another.

In Burke's terms, "Resolution and Independence" is a serious and complicated strategy for pulling oneself out of neurotic depression, and for warding off the real evil eye of psychotic depressive mania. It might operate symbolically for a reader in a comparable situation, but is hardly the simple moral teaching its author thought.

To get at the poem we must look more closely at the climactic revelation and analyze the experience it embodies. This consists of two visionary moments. In the first, in stanza sixteen, the leech gatherer becomes hallucinatory and magical, like a great mystical flow of energy:

> The old Man still stood talking by my side;
> But now his voice to me was like a stream
> Scarce heard; nor word from word could I divide;
> And the whole body of the Man did seem
> Like one whom I had met with in a dream.

In the second, in stanza nineteen, the leech gatherer becomes a timeless recurrence, like Ahasuerus the

Wandering Jew (recall that their friend Jones took him for a Jew):

> In my mind's eye I seemed to see him pace
> About the weary moors continually,
> Wandering about alone and silently.

When he first appears, the leech gatherer is a manifestation of nature like the birds and the hare, an old man by a bare pool:

> As a huge stone is sometimes seen to lie
> Couched on the bald top of an eminence;
> Wonder to all who do the same espy,
> By what means it could thither come, and whence;
> So that it seems a thing endued with sense:
> Like a sea-beast crawled forth, that on a shelf
> Of rock or sand reposeth, there to sun itself.

He soon becomes more insubstantial:

> And, still as I drew near with gentle pace,
> Upon the margin of that moorish flood
> Motionless as a cloud the old Man stood,
> That heareth not the loud winds when they call;
> And moveth all together, if it move at all.

Walter Pater wrote in *Appreciations:*

> The leech-gatherer on the moor, the woman 'stepping westward' are for him natural objects, almost in the same sense as the aged thorn, or the lichened rock on the heath.

Natural objects, however, are not simply that. John Heath-Stubbs reminds us in *Tribute to Wordsworth*, edited by Muriel Spark and Derek Stanford, that for Wordsworth "objects of natural beauty become vehicles of Grace, in the place of the Sacraments of the Church." The old leech gatherer is that, *plus* some sort of incarnation of the divine in the human, and as such he can redeem and "save" as earlier animal nature cannot.

As he is an embodiment of nature and grace, so the old leech gatherer is a figuration of the poet. Wordsworth sees him hunting leeches in a literary metaphor:

> At length, himself unsettling, he the pond
> Stirred with his staff, and fixedly did look
> Upon the muddy water, which he conned,
> As if he had been reading in a book.

His account of the scarcity of leeches is not a business statistic as it is in Wordsworth's encounter with the retired leech gatherer who inspired the poem, but sounds like a poet lamenting the poverty of his poetic inspirations:

> Once I could meet with them on every side;
> But they have dwindled long by slow decay;
> Yet still I persevere, and find them where I may.

The leech gatherer, stirring the leeches about his feet, literally feeding them on his own blood, becomes an incredibly bold metaphor for the poet in his sacrificial role; Chatterton, Burns, or Wordsworth himself, making poetry out of his life's blood. In *Tribute to Wordsworth,* G. S. Fraser writes:

> What Wordsworth had met with, of course, what awed and terrified him in the old leech-gatherer, was a dream image of *himself;* of himself as a lonely, patriarchal, godlike figure.

It would be more accurate, I would submit, to say that Wordsworth had met with a *nightmare* image of himself, godlike not in power but in sacrificial attributes, a suffering savior in fact. By projecting this terrifying role onto the old man, in Burke's terms of symbolic action, Wordsworth can go on writing poetry purged and restored.

More generally still, the leech gatherer is a figuration of man in various aspects. He is a noble image of suffering humanity:

> His body was bent double, feet and head
> Coming together in life's pilgrimage;
> As if some dire constraint of pain, or rage
> Of sickness felt by him in times long past,
> A more than human weight upon his frame had
>   cast.

The old man speaks feebly, but his feeble words are gentle, courteous, solemn, lofty:

> Choice word and measured phrase, above the
>   reach
> Of ordinary men; a stately speech;

Such as grave Livers do in Scotland use,
Religious men, who give to God and man their
dues.

"Being old and poor," homeless, "he had many hardships to endure." In this aspect the leech gatherer is not only a type of sorrowful humanity, but a homeopathic vision of Wordsworth's own possible future of poverty and bleakness. A similar encounter with a poverty-stricken soldier in Book IV of *The Prelude* reassures Wordsworth in his vocation as "A dedicated Spirit." The soldier, like the London beggar in Book VII, functions as a scapegoat figure to carry away the curse of future distress. Lionel Trilling, in *The Liberal Imagination*, takes "Resolution and Independence," which he calls "this great poem," to be the "timely utterance" referred to in the "Ode on Intimations of Immortality," and reads it as an exorcising of anxieties about imagined catastrophes: economic destitution, "natural enough in a man under the stress of approaching marriage, for Wordsworth was to be married in October"; and mental distress. We might add, from the poem's early images, the fear of impotence, and another order of reassurance in the imagery.

Finally, the old man stands for God, or a messenger sent by God. First describing the leech gatherer's appearance, Wordsworth suggests that it might be

by peculiar grace,
A leading from above, a something given.

Concluding the poem in the last stanza, he prays:

> 'God,' said I, 'be my help and stay secure;'

promising to think of the leech gatherer in moments of doubt. James Russell Lowell has emphasized this feature of Wordsworth's poetry in comparison with that of Pope. Lowell writes in "Wordsworth":

> If Pope has made current more epigrams of worldly wisdom, to Wordsworth belongs the nobler praise of having defined for us, and given us for a daily possession, those faint and vague suggestions of other-worldliness of whose gentle ministry with our baser nature the hurry and bustle of life scarcely ever allowed us to be conscious.

In terms of these strongly redemptive features in the central experience of the poem, it is interesting to read Wordsworth's own didactic interpretation. In June, 1802, Sara Hutchinson, the sister of his fiancée, criticized the earlier draft of the poem. Wordsworth wrote to her, and through her to her sister Mary:

> I am exceedingly sorry that the latter part of the Leechgatherer has displeased you, the more so because I cannot take to myself (that being the case) much pleasure or satisfaction in having pleased you in the former part. I will explain to you in prose my feeling in writing that poem and then you will be better able to judge

whether the fault be mine or yours or partly both. I describe myself as having been exalted to the highest pitch of delight by the joyousness and beauty of Nature; and then as depressed, even in the midst of those beautiful objects, to the lowest dejection and despair. A young Poet in the midst of the happiness of Nature is described as overwhelmed by the thought of the miserable reverses which have befallen the happiest of all men, *viz.* Poets. I think of this till I am so deeply impressed with it, that I consider the manner in which I was rescued from my dejection and despair almost as an interposition of Providence. Now whether it was by peculiar grace, A leading from above—A person reading this Poem with feelings like mine will have been awed and controuled, expecting almost something spiritual or supernatural. What is brought forward? 'A lonely place, a Pond,' 'by which an old man *was*, far from all house or home': not *stood*, not *sat*, but *was*—the figure presented in the most naked simplicity possible. This feeling of spirituality or supernaturalness is again referred to as being strong in my mind in this passage. How came he here? thought I, or what can he be doing? I then describe him, whether ill or well is not for me to judge with perfect confidence, but this I can confidently affirm, that though I believe God has given me a strong imagination, I cannot conceive a figure more impressive than that of an old Man like this, the survivor of a Wife and ten children, travelling along among the mountains and all lonely places, carrying with him his own fortitude, and the necessities which an unjust state of society has entailed upon him. You say and Mary (that is you can say no more than that) the poem is very well after the introduction of the old man, this is not true, if it is not more than very well it is very bad—there is no intermediate state. You speak of his speech as tedious: everything is tedious when one does not read with the feelings of the Author. *The Thorn* is tedious to hundreds; and so is *The Idiot Boy* to hundreds. It is in the character of the old man to tell his story, which an impatient reader must necessarily feel as tedious. But, Good God, Such a figure, in such a place; a pious, self-respecting, miserably infirm and [ ] Old Man tell such a tale!

My dear Sara, it is not a matter of indifference whether you are pleased with this figure and his employment; it may be comparatively so, whether you are pleased or not with his Poem; but it is of the utmost importance that you should have had pleasure from contemplating the fortitude, independence, persevering spirit, and the general moral dignity of this old man's character. Your feelings about the Mother, and the Boys with the Butterfly, were not indifferent: it was an affair of whole continents of moral sympathy. I will talk more with you on

> this when we meet—at present, farewell and Heaven for ever bless you.

Dorothy Wordsworth added a scolding note of her own:

> When you happen to be displeased with what you may suppose to be the tendency or moral of any poem which William writes, ask yourself whether you have hit upon the real tendency and true moral, and above all never think that he writes for no reason but merely because a thing happened—and when you feel any poem of his to be tedious, ask yourself in what spirit it was written—whether merely to tell the tale and be through with it, or to illustrate a particular character or truth.

Ironically, Wordsworth appears to have accepted Sara Hutchinson's criticism to the extent of rewriting the poem to leave out the details of the old man's family history that she found tedious, and he probably changed the title to emphasize the significance he thought she had missed.

A glance at Wordsworth's poetic techniques seems in order. The personality of the poet is very much in evidence in "Resolution and Independence," not only as a participant in the meeting, but commenting directly on the experience, as when he says of leech-gathering:

> Employment hazardous and wearisome!

One of Wordsworth's resources is the pun. The pun in "moorish flood" is obviously an extraneous and unintended suggestion, as is "grave livers." However, "be my help and stay secure" is certainly a deliberate ambiguity, and quite a poignant one, in which "stay" is both a noun and an imperative verb addressed to God, and the "resolution" in the title means not only that the old man is resolute but that Wordsworth's trouble has been resolved. When Wordsworth is bad he is terrible, like the lines

> Wonder to all who do the same espy,
> By what means it could thither come, and
>   whence;

quoted earlier, or the terrible flatness in the last stanza:

> And soon with this he other matter blended,
> Cheerfully uttered, with demeanour kind,
> But stately in the main;

When H. A. Taine, in his *History of English Literature*, said of Wordsworth essentially what Wordsworth and his contemporaries said of Pope, that he wrote rhymed prose, Taine had such lines in mind.

Bradley, who called "Resolution and Independence" "the most Wordsworthian of Wordsworth's poems, and the best test of ability to understand him," comments:

> When we read it, we find instead lines of extraordinary grandeur, but, mingled with them,

lines more pedestrian than could be found in an impressive poem from any other hand.

We must remember the extraordinary grandeur as well as the flatness. For me, the grandeur is represented best by the first four lines of stanza seventeen:

> My former thoughts returned: the fear that
> kills;
> And hope that is unwilling to be fed;
> Cold, pain, and labour, and all fleshly ills;
> And mighty Poets in their misery dead.

Herbert Read's *Wordsworth* makes the poet almost an *angst*-ridden Existentialist contemporary with us. He writes:

> All in all, Wordsworth's philosophy is a noble one, and because it was fashioned in an age of disillusionment, and in a mood of almost helpless despair, it is a philosophy that has particular significance for our own age.

It has been charged that Wordsworth restored poetry to natural speech after the artifice of the Augustans, but then developed natural speech into a new kind of artifice. "Artifice," however, is only a somewhat slighting way of saying "art," "craft." If Wordsworth replaced Pope's convention of good sense elegantly put with a convention of passionate feeling baldly put, it is equally a style that can convey the deepest truths of experience.

THE SANCTION for "Resolution and Independence" comes in 1817, with the publication of *Biographia Literaria* by Wordsworth's friend Samuel Taylor Coleridge. This odd book, surely the greatest work of literary criticism in English, is almost impossible to synopsize, since it is an organization of digressions rivaling *Tristram Shandy*. Coleridge explains on the first page:

> I have used the narration chiefly for the purpose of giving a continuity to the work, in part for the sake of the miscellaneous reflections suggested to me by particular events, but still more as introductory to a statement of my principles in Politics, Religion, and Philosophy, and an application of the rules, deduced from philosophical principles, to poetry and criticism.

The book is intellectual autobiography, defense of Wordsworth's poetry, poetics and theory of criticism, and a medley of psychology, philosophy, aesthetics, semantics, and concrete literary criticism, including some of the best we have. In his 1807 letter to Lady Beaumont, Wordsworth wrote:

> Never forget what, I believe, was observed to you by Coleridge, that every great and original writer, in proportion as he is great or original, must himself create the taste by which he is to be relished; he must teach the art by which he is to be seen.

The *Biographia Literaria* is an effort to help Wordsworth's poetry create that taste, but in a deeper purpose Coleridge is using Wordsworth's poetry to create a taste by means of which Coleridge's own poetry, and all later Romantic poetry, may be relished.

The two key words of the *Biographia* are stated in the opening sentence of the celebrated Chapter Fourteen. Coleridge writes:

> During the first year that Mr. Wordsworth and I were neighbours, our conversations turned frequently on the two cardinal points of poetry, the power of exciting the sympathy of the reader by a faithful adherence to the truth of nature, and the power of giving the interest of novelty by the modifying colours of imagination.

Under "nature" Coleridge subsumes all that Johnson does and a great deal more. It means "things of every day" as a subject of poetry, "the natural conversation of men under the influence of natural feelings." It implies a style with "no mark of strained thought, or forced diction, no crowd or turbulence of imagery," at its best; "meanness of language and inanity of thought" at its worst. In this cluster art is "mere artifices of connection or ornament," which "constitute the characteristic falsity in the poetic style of the moderns." Opposed to natural style are "the gaudy affectations of a style which passed current with too many for poetic diction," or "false and showy splendour." Another natural quality for Coleridge, as it was for Johnson, is poetic genius. "I conclude," Coleridge writes, "that Poetic Genius is not only a very delicate but a very rare plant." Poetry is "the natural language of impassioned feeling," and Coleridge writes of Wordsworth: "He has evinced the truth of passion." At the same time, "healthy feelings" are to be accompanied by "a reflecting mind," and Wordsworth "possessed both genius and a powerful intellect." Coleridge even couples "nature" with Johnson's key neo-classical term, and notes Wordsworth's "justifiable preference for the language of nature and of good sense."

Under "imagination," all the transformations of art come in. The basic distinction of the *Biographia* is one Coleridge makes between "fancy" and "imagination," with fancy the lower ornamental faculty, and imagination the high creative quality, as in: "Milton had a highly *imaginative*, Cowley a very *fanciful* mind." Coleridge writes:

> The poet, described in ideal perfection, brings the whole soul of man into activity, with

> the subordination of its faculties to each other according to their relative worth and dignity. He diffuses a tone and spirit of unity, that blends, and (as it were) *fuses*, each into each, by that synthetic and magical power, to which I would exclusively appropriate the name of Imagination.

Coleridge concludes Chapter Fourteen:

> Finally, Good Sense is the Body of poetic genius, Fancy its Drapery, Motion its Life, and Imagination the Soul that is everywhere, and in each; and forms all into one graceful and intelligent whole.

The genius that Wordsworth combines with intellect is actually imagination. Coleridge writes:

> For without his depth of feeling and his imaginative power his *sense* would want its vital warmth and peculiarity; and without his strong sense, his *mysticism* would become *sickly*—mere fog, and dimness!

Wordsworth accepted Coleridge's distinction enough to classify some of his poems in the final collection as "Poems of the Fancy" and some (among them "Resolution and Independence") as "Poems of the Imagination." I. A. Richards, who has written a whole book, *Coleridge on Imagination*, exploring the term, finds that Coleridge and Wordsworth differed in their understanding of the process, if they did not differ in accepting it as a transcendental value.

One of the qualities imagination produces in poetry is Longinus' elevation, poems "of loftier kind," as against "unpleasant sinking from the height." Coleridge remarks of Wordsworth that "the natural tendency of the poet's mind is to great objects and elevated conceptions," adding truthfully but somewhat tactlessly, "He sinks too often and too abruptly." In the cluster of imagination, artifice is not meretricious but the essential of art. Explaining that "a poem of any length neither can be, nor ought to be, all poetry," Coleridge adds:

> Yet if an harmonious whole is to be produced, the remaining parts must be preserved in keeping with the poetry; and this can be no otherwise effected than by such a studied selection and artificial arrangement, as will partake of one, though not a peculiar property of poetry.

Here we get to Coleridge's definition of a poem, which reads:

> A poem is that species of composition, which is opposed to works of science, by proposing for its *immediate* object pleasure, not truth; and from all other species—(having *this* object in common with it)—it is discriminated by proposing to itself such delight from the *whole*, as is compatible with a distinct gratification from each component *part*.

Coleridge later criticizes some of Wordsworth's more didactic poetry, "inasmuch as it proposes *truth* for its immediate object, instead of *pleasure*." Wordsworth's own famous definition of a poem, in the preface to the second edition of *Lyrical Ballads*, as taking its origin from "emotion recollected in tranquillity," but gradually replacing the tranquillity with a semblance of the original emotion, is entirely concerned with the poet's state; Coleridge has gone back to Aristotle's concern with the aim or object of the aesthetic process. Coleridge's definition of "poetic faith" as the "willing suspension of disbelief for the moment," makes it clear that the imaginative process goes on in the reader too.

Coleridge's greatest specific concern with Wordsworth is with the language of his poetry. His quarrel is with Wordsworth's stated preference in the preface to the *Lyrical Ballads* for "the language of real life," which he professed to find only in rural surroundings. As Coleridge points out, many of Wordsworth's poems are written "in the impassioned, lofty, and sustained diction, which is characteristic of his genius." Furthermore, Coleridge observes, some of the finest English poetry has the excellence of simple diction without any rustic pretensions, instancing Chaucer, Spenser, Waller and Herbert. Like Bradley, Coleridge finds "Resolution and Independence" "especially characteristic of the author," in regard to its defects as well as its excellences. His later summary of Wordsworth's excellences, however, clearly shows why he valued

"Resolution and Independence" so highly. They are:

> An austere purity of language both grammatically and logically; in short a perfect appropriateness of the words to the meaning.
>
> A correspondent weight and sanity of the Thoughts and Sentiments,—won, not from books; but—from the poet's own meditative observation.
>
> The sinewy strength and originality of single lines and paragraphs.
>
> The perfect truth of nature in his images and descriptions as taken immediately from nature, and proving a long and genial intimacy with the very spirit which gives the physiognomic expression of all the works of nature. Like a green field reflected in a calm and perfectly transparent lake, the image is distinguished from the reality only by its greater softness and lustre.
>
> A meditative pathos, a union of deep and subtle thought with sensibility; a sympathy with man as man.

By these criteria, "Resolution and Independence" is a great poem and Wordsworth a great poet. Coleridge concludes, exactly like Johnson on Pope, that his defects are insignificant in comparison with his beauties. For our time, J. K. Stephen has caught the Wordsworthian contradiction neatly. He writes:

Two voices are there: one is of the deep;
It learns the storm cloud's thunderous melody,
Now roars, now murmurs with the changing sea,
Now bird-like pipes, now closes soft in sleep:
And one is of an old half-witted sheep
Which bleats inarticulate monotony,
And indicates that two and one are three,
That grass is green, lakes damp, and mountains steep:
And, Wordsworth, both are thine. . . .

Coleridge's image for the same paradox is considerably more charitable. He writes:

> In short, that his only disease is the being out of his element; like the swan, that, having amused himself, for a while, with crushing the weeds on the river's bank, soon returns to his own majestic movements on its reflecting and sustaining surface.

By Coleridge's standards, Wordsworth at his best is the truest poetry, and his natural element was the best.

IV

Modern Literature

THE STANDARD poem for Victorian England is not a work of the nineteenth century, but *Paradise Lost*, an epic by John Milton, published in 1667. It tells the story of the temptation and Fall of Adam and Eve in paradise, and, by means of flashbacks and flash-forwards, manages to cover most of the Bible. *Paradise Lost* is written in blank verse, as Milton explains in an indignant prefatory note:

> The measure is English Heroic Verse without Rime, as that of Homer in Greek, and of Virgil in Latin; Rime being no necessary Adjunct or true Ornament of Poem or good Verse, in longer Works especially, but the Invention of a barbarous Age, to set off wretched matter and lame Meeter; grac't indeed since by the use of some famous modern Poets, carried

> away by Custom, but much to their own vexation, hindrance, and constraint, to express many things otherwise, and for the most part worse, then else they would have exprest them.

Milton's intention for many years had been to write an epic of King Arthur and the Round Table, but as early as 1641, when he began his career of religious pamphleteering with the *Treatise on Reformation,* he seems to have decided that a sacred subject was better suited to his talents, and certainly to his prejudices. In addition to the Bible, Milton's sources included several earlier Latin poems on the subject, the best-known of them Grotius' *Adamus Exsul. Paradise Lost* was first published in ten books, and was expanded to twelve for the second edition in 1674 by splitting two books in half and adding a few introductory lines.

The aim of the poem, as it boldly announces at the start, is to "justify the ways of God to men." Milton's model is primarily the *Iliad*, as his opening lines make clear:

> Of Man's first disobedience and the fruit
> Of that forbidden tree, whose mortal taste
> Brought death into the world and all our woe,
> With loss of Eden, till one greater Man
> Restore us and regain the blissful seat,
> Sing heav'nly Muse . . .

The Muse is explained as the inspirer of Moses, that is, the Holy Ghost, but she sounds more like one of the Nine, and Book Seven, before it tells the story of the creation, frankly invokes Urania, the muse of astronomy. Homeric reminiscences are everywhere. God weighs the issue of the battle between the hosts of heaven and hell in a golden scale, as Zeus does the battles at Troy. The vision of the future given Adam in Book Eleven is as much like the Shield of Achilles as possible.

The poem is studded with Homeric similes, some as inappropriate as Homer's worst, some perfect miniatures and foreshadowings of the poem's development, like the "fruit" and "woe" of the invocation. As do the best of Homer's, some of the similes have an extremely complex relation to the poem's themes, as for example one for Satan's flight in Book Two:

> As when far off at sea a fleet descried
> Hangs in the clouds, by equinoctial winds
> Close sailing from Bengala, or the Isles
> Of Ternate and Tidore, whence merchants bring
> Their spicy drugs: they on the trading flood
> Through the wide Aethiopian to the Cape
> Ply, stemming nightly toward the pole: so seem'd
> Far off the flying fiend.

William Empson in *Some Versions of Pastoral* has explored some of the relevancies here with his usual brilliance:

> The ships ply nightly because Satan was in the darkness visible of Hell; are far off so that they hang like a mirage and seem flying like Satan (the word *ply*, sounding like 'fly,' ekes this out); and are going towards the Pole because Satan (from inside) is going towards the top of the concave wall of Hell. They carry spices, like those of Paradise, because they stand for paganism and earthly glory, for all that Milton had retained contact with after renouncing and could pile up into the appeal of Satan; Satan is like a merchant because Eve is to exchange these goods for her innocence; and like a fleet rather than one ship because of the imaginative wealth of polytheism and the variety of the world.

When the simile reappears in Book Four, "Sabean odours from the spicy shore" are used for Satan smelling the perfumes of paradise, the tempter tempted. Even a kind of Homeric epithet is present. Dawn comes like Homer's rosy-fingered lady, Adam has a series of epithets like "our primitive great sire," and Satan incarnate in the serpent an even more extensive series, including "the spirited sly snake," "the wily adder," "th'infernal Serpent," "the dire snake," and "that false worm." God addresses his angels in one of Milton's ringing lines: "Thrones, Dominations, Princedoms, Virtues, Powers," and Satan then addresses the forces of hell with the same sequence of epithets.

The poem's long prophecies of the future resemble the *Aeneid* more than the *Iliad*, as do some of the didactic passages, and the descriptions of nature in paradise are quite Vergilian in quality. There are many Shakespearian reminiscences, including such phrases lifted intact as the beautiful "This pendant world" from *Measure for Measure*, and the first appearance of Eve to Adam will remind us of Cleopatra in *Antony and Cleopatra:*

> Grace was in all her steps, heav'n in her eye.

Inevitably, the Authorized Version of the Bible overshadows all the other sources and analogues. The marvelous rolling catalogues of names remind us of Bible genealogies, and even a line or two summons up magic:

> Jousted in Aspramont or Montalban,
> Damasco, or Marocco, or Trebisond,

Milton uses the language of the English Bible to tell its stories. When he finds contradictions in it, as in the two Flood stories in Genesis, in one of which Noah takes two of each beast into the ark, in the other seven each of the clean beasts, Milton marches boldly on: "Came sevens, and pairs, and enter'd in." Sometimes his use of Bible language is only an echo, as when fallen Adam challenges God in a voice like Job's:

> Did I request thee, Maker, from my clay,
> To mould me man?

Often it is the language of St. Paul in I Corinthians. God tells his Son:

> As in him perish all men, so in thee,
> As from a second root, shall be restor'd.

Milton echoes another passage when he writes of Adam and Eve in a line that has infuriated feminists:

> He for God only, she for God in him.

Even Satan parodies I Corinthians to tempt Eve, telling her of the apple:

> in the day
> Ye eat thereof, your eyes that seem so clear,
> Yet are but dim, shall perfectly be then
> Open'd and clear'd.

and

> So ye shall die perhaps, by putting off
> Human, to put on Gods.

Paradise Lost was originally planned as a tragedy, and two of Milton's outlines for it in dramatic form survive. The main features our epic retains from these early dramatic sketches are two allegorical figures, Sin and Death, and a concentration on character and speech that seems remarkably theatrical. The most attractive character, at least in the early books, is Satan. We meet him in the first book as a mixture of "obdurate pride and stedfast hate," mouthing defiance:

yet not for those,
Nor what the potent victor in his rage
Can else inflict, do I repent, or change,
Though chang'd in outward lustre, that fix'd mind
And high disdain from sense of injur'd merit,
That with the Mightiest rais'd me to contend,
And to the fierce contention brought along
Innumerable force of Spirits arm'd,
That durst dislike his reign; and, me preferring,
His utmost power with adverse power oppos'd
In dubious battel on the plains of heav'n,
And shook his throne. What though the field be lost?
All is not lost; th' unconquerable will,
And study of revenge, immortal hate
And courage never to submit or yield,
And what is else not to be overcome;

From this high quality Satan never falls off, gaining "resolution from despair"; his slogan: "Better to reign in hell, than serve in heav'n." Enthroned above his hosts, he is, Milton says, "by merit rais'd/ To that bad eminence." Satan is a keen psychologist, like Marlowe's Mephistophilis, recognizing the inner nature of all that the poem presents as outer: "My self am hell." Like the Faustus of Marlowe's source, he is an "unsatiable speculator," and watching Adam and Eve in paradise, thinks:

One fatal tree there stands of Knowledge call'd
Forbidden them to taste: knowledge forbidden.

Suspicious, reasonless. Why should their Lord
Envy them that? can it be sin to know?
Can it be death?

Satan appeals to his followers to resist God's tyranny as to a free and independent yeomanry, addressing them as "Natives and sons of heav'n." When Satan in the ninth book stands "stupidly good," disarmed by the innocence and beauty of Eve, he is saved by "the hot hell that always in him burns."

Against this sort of dramatic competition, God cannot do very well. God sometimes speaks like Aristotle's rhetorician, exclaiming of Adam's anticipated Fall:

Whose fault?
Whose but his own? ingrate, he had of me
All he could have; I made him just and right,
Sufficient to have stood, though free to fall.

God is least dramatically interesting, although orthodox in Judaeo-Christian theology, when he explains:

necessity and chance
Approach not me, and what I will is fate.

Things improve when Milton forgets that, and makes God limited by his own decrees and by the Fates, like Zeus in the *Iliad*, helplessly watching his son Sarpedon die. There is a poignancy in God's accepting the same fate for *his* Son, "The rigid satisfaction, death for death," and in his inability to grant Jesus' plea that Adam remain in paradise, because "The law I gave to nature him forbids." William Blake said in "The Marriage of Heaven and Hell":

> The reason Milton wrote in fetters when he wrote of Angels & God, and at liberty when he wrote of Devils & Hell is because he was a true Poet and of the Devil's party without knowing it.

It is not really profitable to consider Milton a secret Satanist, although we must recognize what Maud Bodkin in *Archetypal Patterns in Poetry* called Milton's "profoundly felt division and tension of the soul between loyalty and revolt." In literary terms, good is intrinsically less interesting than evil, and an omnipotent character is dramatically impossible. God the Son in *Paradise Lost* is totally uninteresting, an endless affirmation of perfect love and goodness, as Christianity requires him to be. We can, however, hardly ask that Milton risk his immortal soul by limiting God's powers and flawing Christ's nature to produce a more effective dramatic conflict and to keep Satan from stealing the show.

With Adam and Eve, the poet has more leeway. Adam starts as a prig, smiling down on Eve "with superior love," and, when she has a bad dream, lecturing her on psychology. In Book Eight his arguments to God in favor of a mate are specious and rhetorical in the worst sense. Adam begins to come out of it when he tells Raphael that although he understands logically that woman is the inferior,

> yet when I approach
> Her loveliness, so absolute she seems
> And in her self complete, so well to know
> Her own, that what she wills to do or say
> Seems wisest, virtuousest, discreetest, best:

When Eve eats the apple, Adam nobly and bravely decides (and this is Milton's boldest revision of the Genesis story) to eat it out of love in order to share her fate. Adam says:

> If death
> Consort with thee, death is to me as life;

Like Antony, he eats the fruit of love:

> Against his better knowledge, not deceiv'd,
> But fondly overcome with female charm.

To match Adam's superiority, Eve begins in happy subservience. She addresses him:

> God is thy law, thou mine; to know no more
> Is woman's happiest knowledge and her praise.

By Book Nine, Eve has acquired enough spunk to answer Adam's demand that she stay close by him to avoid temptation with Milton's own arguments. She asks:

> And what is faith, love, virtue, unassay'd
> Alone, without exterior help sustain'd?

In *Areopagitica*, his defense of a free press published in 1644, Milton had written:

> I cannot praise a fugitive and cloistered virtue, unexercised and unbreathed, that never sallies out and sees her adversary, but slinks out of the race, where that immortal garland is to be run for, not without dust and heat.

Milton then addresses Eve in his own voice:

> O much deceiv'd, much failing, hapless Eve.

Deceived and failing she may be, but not hapless. She has eaten the apple in part to gain equality, "for inferior who is free?" She then resolves to pull Adam down into fate and death with her, not out of Satan's wickedness ("But ever to do ill our sole delight") but out of the same love to which Adam eventually responds:

> Confirm'd then I resolve,
> Adam shall share with me in bliss or woe:
> So dear I love him, that with him all deaths
> I could endure; without him live no life.

The angels are inevitably a dull lot. Raphael lectures Adam on "temperance over appetite" in regard to knowledge, teaches him elementary astronomy, and even does a little marriage counseling, advising him to dominate his wife and not give in to that unworthy feeling that she is his equal or superior. Michael preaches physical temperance, "the rule of not too much," and like a good YMCA secretary tells Adam that evil comes "from man's effeminate slackness." When Adam and Eve are told the compensation for their miseries in the last book, that Christ will be born from their seed, to avenge them on Satan and establish the Kingdom (the doctrine of *Felix Culpa* or Fortunate Fall), it merely underlines their superiority to the angels, the tragic necessity that without a fall there can be no rise. In their freedom to choose evil, they are even freer than God, whom Eve accurately calls:

> Our great Forbidder, safe with all his spies
> About him.

Herbert Weisinger, in *Tragedy and the Paradox of the Fortunate Fall*, writes of "Milton's conviction that to be truly man, one must be capable of choice, and more, must be capable of bearing the burden of that choice." Man, that is, or epic hero.

The true hero of the poem is the poet. Milton keeps ten thousand blank verse lines from monotony by remarkably controlled variation, putting the caesura almost everywhere in the line, and reversing and varying every metrical foot. The rhythm of the diction interplays with the metrics. Sometimes we have ten monosyllables making perfect iambs:

> And swims, or sinks, or wades, or creeps, or flies.

Sometimes ten monosyllables produce as many as eight accents:

> Rocks, caves, lakes, fens, bogs, dens, and
> shades of death.

Or we may have as few as three words:

> Unrespited, unpitied, unrepriev'd.

If Milton needs an extra foot, he is shameless about doubling a negative, so that "mortal" becomes "unimmortal," or augmenting a plural, so that "Chinese" becomes "Chineses." Sometimes a line is pathetically weak because it consists largely of prepositions:

> Direct against which open'd from beneath.

At other times four heavy beats make it like a hammer:

> To chains of darkness and th' undying worm.

If that is not strong enough, Milton will alliterate the four heavy words:

> Defac'd, deflower'd, and now to death devote.

He is uncannily sensitive to sound. In the passage in Book Nine where Adam permits Eve to go off alone, noting only the consonants, we can hear resolution in the p's and b's, moans in the w's, then the hissing of the snake in the s's and a false assurance in the final balanced line:

> These paths and bowers doubt not but our joint
> hands
> Will keep from wilderness with ease, as wide
> As we need walk, till younger hands ever long
> Assist us: but if much converse perhaps

Thee satiate, to short absence I could yield:
For solitude sometimes is best society,
And short retirement urges sweet return.

Some of Milton's ideas derive from what Coleridge would call the fancy. The hellhound children of Sin, who creep back into her womb when they are disturbed, are an unlovely example. The elephant who entertains Adam and Eve in Eden by wreathing "his lithe proboscis" is a more charming illustration. Often we are not sure whether we are laughing with or at Milton, as when Adam serves the angel Raphael a fruit banquet in Paradise and the poet adds the reassuring comment: "No fear lest dinner cool." The account of Satan's wound in Book Six seems almost as whimsical as the parody it inspired, the poor halved sylph in "The Rape of the Lock":

but th' ethereal substance clos'd
Not long divisible, and from the gash
A stream of nectarous humor issuing flow'd
Sanguine, such as celestial spirits may bleed.

Satan's invention of artillery is a bold stroke, but a bold stroke of the fancy, and it is not improved when the poet conjectures that someone might invent the same devilment for mankind in the future. We get a similar conceit more charmingly when Adam decides that Noah's rainbow is some sort of waterproof binding God has put on the clouds.

At other times Milton's effects can only be called truly imaginative. A staggering example has Satan call in Book Two for a volunteer who will venture "the dark unbottom'd infinite abyss" to earth. When no one dares, he proudly volunteers himself. This scene then repeats in Book Three when God calls for a volunteer who will die to redeem man, and when no one dares, God's Son volunteers. Christian theology has always understood that God's incarnation and atonement are consequent to man's fall, but only Milton's poem has dared suggest that the scheme was initiated in hell rather than in heaven, and that Satan was Christ's prototype. We get another example of high poetic imagination in Book Seven, in Raphael's account of the creation, where Milton literally sees the earth becoming flesh:

> The grassy clods now calv'd, now half appear'd
> The tawny lion, pawing to get free
> His hinder parts, then springs as broke from bonds,
> And rampant shakes his brinded mane.

Adam's vision of the distempers his sin has brought into the world has the loony imagination and power of a Bosch picture:

> Immediately a place
> Before his eyes appear'd, sad, noisome, dark,
> A lazar-house it seem'd, wherein were laid
> Numbers of all diseas'd, all maladies
> Of ghastly spasm, or racking torture, qualms
> Of heart-sick agony, all feverous kinds,
> Convulsions, epilepsies, fierce catarrhs,

Intestine stone and ulcer, colic pangs,
Daemoniac frenzy, moping melancholy,
And moon-struck madness, pining atrophy,
Marasmus, and wide-wasting pestilence,
Dropsies, and asthmas, and joint-racking
rheums.

The theology of the poem gives Milton opportunity for all sorts of personal intrusion. As he was Arian, believing the Son less than the Father although of the same divine substance, and Arminian, believing in free will against predestination, so *Paradise Lost* is Arian and Arminian. That is fair enough, but it is probably unfair to have the devils in hell debate predestination and foreknowledge like a lot of Calvinists at Geneva, or to have God assure the reader of the truth of Milton's opinions regarding the freedom of the will, grace, and election. When the angels sing in heaven, they sing Milton's theology of the Father and of the Son, not omitting an iota. Milton's tone toward rival theologians is not outstanding for Christian charity, as in the lines when Satan comes to Eden:

So clomb this first grand thief into GOD's fold;
So since into his church lewd hirelings climb.

There is a nasty Dantesque quality to his vision of Roman Catholics in a windy limbo:

then might ye see
Cowls, hood, and habits with their wearers tost
And flutter'd into rags; then reliques, beads,

Indulgences, dispenses, pardons, bulls,
The sport of winds: all these upwhirl'd aloft
Fly o'er the backside of the world far off,
Into a limbo large and broad, since call'd
The Paradise of fools.

We see and hear Milton all through the poem. His impatient voice breaks into the council of hell:

O shame to men! devil with devil damn'd
Firm concord holds, men only disagree
Of creatures rational, though under hope
Of heav'nly grace; and God proclaiming peace,
Yet live in hatred, enmity, and strife
Among themselves, and levy cruel wars,
Wasting the earth, each other to destroy:
As if, which might induce us to accord,
Man had not hellish foes enow besides,
That day and night for his destruction wait.

We hear Milton again, in response to his own marital difficulties, celebrating connubial love. When Abdiel stands alone against Satan's hosts, is praised by God for maintaining "the cause of truth" against "Universal reproach," and eventually acquires a "sect" to support him, Milton is not lurking far in the background. The proem to Book Seven is a touching vision of the poet at the Restoration, "fall'n on evil days," and the introduction to Book Nine a proudly humble account of his genesis of the epic, "long choosing and beginning late." We can even see Milton as Satan in Book Nine, beholding paradise like a Londoner:

> As one who long in populous city pent
> Where houses thick and sewers annoy the air,
> Forth issuing on a summer's morn to breathe
> Among the pleasant villages and farms
> Adjoin'd.

The most meaningful personal touches are the references to Milton's blindness. Book Three begins with a beautiful apostrophe to "holy light," explaining that the poet is blind, and praying for a compensating inward light of understanding. In the poem, heaven is always bright light and hell awful dark, and Satan curses the sun, as Milton might in some moods, for reminding him of what he has lost. Light is invariably good and dark bad in *Paradise Lost;* dark extinguishes life itself while light disperses evil. Adam's vision of Noah in Book Eleven as "the only son of light/ In a dark age" is Milton's final self-vision in the poem, and we know that his prayer for a compensating light has been answered to his own satisfaction. If the theme of the poem is an intensification of the theme of *All for Love*, paradise itself well lost for love (but only temporarily), the work is probably not a tragedy, but what Isabel Gamble MacCaffrey calls it in *Paradise Lost as "Myth,"* a "divine comedy." If we take Milton to be its true protagonist, however, it is a genuine tragic action, with the poet suffering an interior fall from the heaven of light, but like blind Teiresias and Oedipus, gaining the clearer perception of the seer. Adam falls in the poem that Christ may rise, but Milton falls by means of the poem in order that as a poet he himself may rise.

THE POETICS that establishes *Paradise Lost* as the standard in the last century is Matthew Arnold's essay "The Study of Poetry," published in 1880 as a general introduction to an edition of *The English Poets*. It redefines the nature and function of poetry, proposes a test for distinguishing poetic quality, surveys English poetry up to Arnold's own century in terms of that test, and revalues some reputations.

The definition Arnold proposes is that poetry is a criticism of life, specifically "a criticism of life under the conditions fixed for such a criticism by the laws of poetic truth and poetic beauty." The year before, in his introduction to *The Poems of Wordsworth*, Arnold had defined "the noble and profound application of ideas to life" as "the most essential part of poetic greatness," and had praised Wordsworth over other poets by that criterion. He wrote:

> Where, then, is Wordsworth's superiority? It is here; he deals with more of *life* than they do; he deals with *life*, as a whole, more powerfully.

In "The Study of Poetry," Arnold goes on to say that as a criticism of life, poetry is a consolation and a stay. He adds:

> But the consolation and stay will be of power in proportion to the power of the criticism of life. And the criticism of life will be of power in proportion as the poetry conveying it is excellent rather than inferior, sound rather than unsound or half-sound, true rather than untrue or half-true.

"The best poetry is what we want," he insists. "The greatness of the great poets," Arnold continues, "the power of their criticism of life, is that their virtue is sustained." In *Culture and Anarchy* in 1869, Arnold defined the necessary aim as "to make the best that has been thought and known in the world current everywhere." By 1880 this is poetry, great poetry. It is also classic poetry, which Arnold defines in terms that would have surprised a long line of critics in earlier centuries:

> He is a real classic, if his work belongs to the class of the very best (for this is the true and right meaning of the word *classic, classical*).

Chaucer, for example, although his poetry is "high criticism of life," "is not one of the great classics," he cannot attain the highest reaches. Gray, on the other hand, sometimes makes it. Arnold writes:

> He is the scantiest and frailest of classics in our poetry, but he is a classic.

What the great classics have in their criticism of life is the quality Arnold calls "high seriousness." He gets the term from Aristotle's statement in the *Poetics* that poetry possesses a higher truth and a higher seriousness than history. "The substance and matter of the best poetry," Arnold writes, "acquire their special character from possessing, in an eminent degree, truth and seriousness." What Chaucer's poetry lacks, and Gray's poetry sometimes attains, is this "high and excellent seriousness," the characteristic of the great classics. When he is rejecting Dryden and Pope as classics of our poetry, to accept them as "classics of our prose," Arnold quotes examples, and comments:

> But do you ask me whether such verse proceeds from men with an adequate poetic criticism of life, from men whose criticism of life has a high seriousness, or even, without that high seriousness, has poetic largeness, freedom, insight, benignity? Do you ask me whether the application of ideas to life in the verse of these men, often a powerful application, no doubt, is a powerful *poetic* application? Do you ask me whether the poetry of these men has either the matter or the inseparable manner of such an adequate poetic criticism . . . ?

High seriousness is "born of absolute sincerity," and Arnold cannot quite bring himself to credit it to Dryden and Pope.

The test of high seriousness, and of the poetic

greatness that follows from it, is Arnold's touchstone method. He explains:

> Indeed there can be no more useful help for discovering what poetry belongs to the class of the truly excellent, and can therefore do us most good, than to have always in one's mind lines and expressions of the great masters, and to apply them as a touchstone to other poetry. Of course we are not to require this other poetry to resemble them; it may be very dissimilar. But if we have any tact we shall find them, when we have lodged them well in our minds, an infallible touchstone for detecting the presence or absence of high poetic quality, and also the degree of this quality, in all other poetry which we may place beside them. Short passages, even single lines, will serve our turn quite sufficiently.

He then quotes as his touchstones three brief passages from the *Iliad*, three of Dante's, two of Shakespeare's, and three from *Paradise Lost*. Arnold explains:

> These few lines, if we have tact and can use them, are enough even of themselves to keep clear and sound our judgments about poetry, to save us from fallacious estimates of it, to conduct us to a real estimate.
>
> The specimens I have quoted differ widely from one another, but they have in common

this: the possession of the very highest poetical quality. If we are thoroughly penetrated by their power, we shall find that we have acquired a sense enabling us, whatever poetry may be laid before us, to feel the degree in which a high poetical quality is present or wanting there. Critics give themselves great labor to draw out what in the abstract constitutes the characters of a high quality of poetry. It is much better simply to have recourse to concrete examples;—to take specimens of poetry of the high, the very highest quality, and to say: The characters of a high quality of poetry are what is expressed *there*. They are far better recognized by being felt in the verse of the master, than by being perused in the prose of the critic. Nevertheless if we are urgently pressed to give some critical account of them, we may safely, perhaps, venture on laying down, not indeed how and why the characters arise, but where and in what they arise. They are in the matter and substance of the poetry, and they are in its manner and style. Both of these, the substance and matter on the one hand, the style and manner on the other, have a mark, an accent, of high beauty, worth, and power. But if we are asked to define this mark and accent in the abstract, our answer must be: No, for we should thereby be darkening the question, not clearing it. The mark and accent are as given by the substance and matter of that

> poetry, by the style and manner of that poetry, and of all other poetry which is akin to it in quality.

Later in the essay two Chaucer touchstones are added to the equipment, showing "charm" and "virtue" if not high seriousness.

Paradise Lost is thus for Arnold a criticism of life possessing high seriousness, and a source of touchstones ranking with Homer, Dante and Shakespeare. Otherwise "The Study of Poetry" scarcely mentions Milton. In his historical account of English poetry, Arnold skips the great age between Chaucer and Dryden with the comment:

> For my present purpose I need not dwell on our Elizabethan poetry, or on the continuation and close of this poetry in Milton. We all of us profess to be agreed in the estimate of this poetry; we all of us recognize it as great poetry, our greatest, and Shakespeare and Milton as our poetical classics. The real estimate, here, has universal currency.

In some of Arnold's other essays we can get more detail. In "Milton" he is again coupled with Shakespeare as the highest standard of English excellence, and is even placed above Shakespeare. Arnold writes:

> If to our English race an inadequate sense for perfection of work is a real danger, if the discipline of respect for a high and flawless excel-

lence is peculiarly needed by us, Milton is of all our gifted men the best lesson, the most salutary influence. In the sure and flawless perfection of his rhythm and diction he is an admirable as Virgil or Dante, and in this respect he is unique amongst us. No one else in English literature and art possesses the like distinction.

Thomson, Cowper, Wordsworth, all of them good poets who have studied Milton, followed Milton, adopted his form, fail in their diction and rhythm if we try them by that high standard of excellence maintained by Milton constantly. From style really high and pure Milton never departs; their departures from it are frequent.

Shakespeare is divinely strong, rich, and attractive. But sureness of perfect style Shakespeare himself does not possess. I have heard a politician express wonder at the treasures of political wisdom in a certain celebrated scene in *Troilus and Cressida;* for my part I am at least equally moved to wonder at the fantastic and false diction in which Shakespeare has in that scene clothed them. Milton, from one end of *Paradise Lost* to the other, is in his diction and rhythm constantly a great artist in the great style.

In "Wordsworth," Arnold complains:

It might seem that Nature not only gave him the matter for his poem, but wrote his poem

> for him. He has no style. He was too conversant with Milton not to catch at times his master's manner, and he has fine Miltonic lines; but he has no assured poetical style of his own, like Milton.

In this picture of Shakespeare as divine but unsteady, and Wordsworth as nature rather than style, we can hear the criteria of Ben Jonson, but the criteria now are romantic rather than classic. Arnold takes the term "high seriousness" from Aristotle, but his touchstone lines of highest eloquence show that he is using it to the purposes of Longinus. The voice is Jacob's voice, but the hands are the hands of Esau.

We can understand the touchstone method and its limitations better if we take a closer look at one of Arnold's touchstones from Milton. He quotes "the exquisite close to the loss of Proserpine, the loss

> . . . which cost Ceres all that pain
> To seek her through the world."

These lines come in Book Four and are part of our first vision of Eden, a comparison with beautiful scenes from pagan mythology. The passage reads:

> Not that fair field
> Of Enna, where Proserpine gathering flow'rs,
> Herself a fairer flow'r, by gloomy Dis
> Was gather'd, which cost Ceres all that pain

> To seek her through the world; nor that sweet grove
> Of Daphne by Orontes and th' inspir'd
> Castalian spring might with this paradise
> Of Eden strive; . . .

They are, as Arnold recognizes, perhaps the most beautiful and moving lines in *Paradise Lost*, and one of the high points of English poetry. But Ceres' pain is moving only because her maiden daughter or aspect, gathering flowers, has been herself gathered by gloomy Dis and taken down into the underworld, in lines that Arnold omits, and because both actions are representative of Milton's story, not decorative. What was planted in Book Four is harvested in Book Nine, Proserpine's flowers are Eve's fruit, and Ceres' pain is man's woe.

John Bailey, in *Milton*, explains the "amazing beauty" of the lines by "the way in which the emotional significance of the whole poem converges upon them." Maud Bodkin, in *Archetypal Patterns in Poetry*, beautifully explains some of this:

> When the tempter appears, to lead Eve to the fruit of that forbidden tree whose taste 'brought death into the world,' he finds her, as Proserpine was found by gloomy Dis, among the flowers, herself the 'fairest unsupported flower.' The pattern is evidently reproduced deliberately by Milton, and one discerns in it, I think, the kind of significance I have called

archetypal. As Proserpine moved in beauty through the flowery field of Enna, a symbol of transient spring loveliness threatened by the powers of the underworld—of dark, cold, and death—so Milton's Eve also stands amid flowers, a symbol of the frailty of earthly joy and loveliness before the Powers of Evil. It is as though the poet's feeling divined the relation of the concepts of Heaven and Hell to the images of spring's beauty and of the darkness under the earth whence beauty comes forth and to which it returns. In the communicated experience, at all events, one finds, through this binding of the tale to the myth-image, that the pattern stands clear, of Satan struggling upwards from his tremendous cavern below the realm of Chaos, to waylay the flower-like Eve in her walled Paradise and make her an inmate of his Hell, even as Pluto rose from beneath the earth to carry off Proserpine from her flowery meadow.

With this background, in this context, Ceres' pain seeking Proserpine through the world is all the pain of Adam following his love (like Orpheus) down into darkness and death, all the pain of Christ suffering on the Cross to redeem mankind, all the pain of man's lifelong quest for radiance and joy, all the pain of the life cycle of birth, growth, decay, death, and rebirth. Arnold leaves out too much. As a touchstone, in short, nothing less than the whole poem will do, perhaps nothing less than all of literature and life.

In the touchstone doctrine, I think, we get an insight into why Arnold's own poetry fragments so readily. Lines written almost a century ago seem of vital, prophetic relevance for our time. We think of the lines from "Dover Beach":

> And we are here as on a darkling plain
> Swept with confused alarms of struggle and
> flight,
> Where ignorant armies clash by night.

or from "The Grande Chartreuse":

> Wandering between two worlds, one dead,
> The other powerless to be born.

When we read them in the context of their poems, however, these great Miltonic lines are diminished rather than augmented. Essentially, Arnold has written touchstones without the poems.

The function of poetry, as Arnold sees it, is nothing less than replacing religion, the Sea of Faith that has ebbed in "Dover Beach." "The strongest part of our religion today is its unconscious poetry," he writes. The definition of culture in *Culture and Anarchy* as "a study of harmonious perfection" makes it a religious exercise, like a Buddhist or Taoist meditation. Arnold writes in "The Study of Poetry":

> We should conceive of poetry worthily, and more highly than it has been the custom to con-

> ceive of it. We should conceive of it as capable of higher uses, and called to higher destinies, than those which in general men have assigned to it hitherto. More and more mankind will discover that we have to turn to poetry to interpret life for us, to console us, to sustain us. Without poetry, our science will appear incomplete; and most of what now passes with us for religion and philosophy will be replaced by poetry.

The effect of poetry, he explains in "Milton," "resides chiefly in the refining and elevation wrought in us by the high and rare excellence of the great style." In *Culture and Anarchy* Arnold quotes Swift's tribute in the *Battle of the Books* to the ancient writers imaged as bees, bringing home honey and wax, and thus furnishing man with "the two noblest of things, which are sweetness and light." Arnold adds: "The perfection of human nature is sweetness and light." Poetry will thus refine us morally, "do us most good," as Aristotle believed. But as Aristotle added, and Coleridge reaffirmed, it can only do that as a secondary aim by succeeding in its primary aim, which is giving pleasure. "The great thing for us," Arnold writes of the classic poet in "The Study of Poetry," "is to feel and enjoy his work as deeply as ever we can." He adds:

> This is what is salutary, this is what is formative; this is the great benefit to be got from the study of poetry.

The last paragraph begins:

> At any rate the end to which the method and the estimate are designed to lead, and from leading to which, if they do lead to it, they get their whole value,—the benefit of being able clearly to feel and deeply to enjoy the best, the truly classic, in poetry,—is an end, let me say it once more at parting, of supreme importance.

Ultimately the end is feeling and enjoying, and *Paradise Lost* is the standard because feeling and enjoying its high seriousness entails moral elevation.

A GOOD example of the CHALLENGE to this standard and poetics comes in 1918 with the publication of "Sweeney Among the Nightingales" by the thirty-year-old Thomas Stearns Eliot. It is a sequence of ten iambic tetrameter quatrains, each rhymed on the second and fourth lines. We know nothing of the poem's occasion. It is a complex and opaque work, not readily paraphrased. Suffice to say that it tells of Sweeney, an earthy character who appears in several other Eliot poems, threatened by violence in some sort of dive, and like Pope's "Rape of the Lock" and Wordsworth's "Resolution and

Independence," establishes wider significances for its relatively trivial events.

We should first note that after all the elevation of Arnold's slogans, Eliot's poem is defiantly low. The scene appears to be a bar frequented by prostitutes, and public behavior there is somewhat indecorous. We are introduced to the protagonist in the first stanza:

> Apeneck Sweeney spreads his knees
> Letting his arms hang down to laugh,
> The zebra stripes along his jaw
> Swelling to maculate giraffe.

The next character enters in the third stanza without much concern for appearances:

> The person in the Spanish cape
> Tries to sit on Sweeney's knees
>
> Slips and pulls the table cloth
> Overturns a coffee-cup,
> Reorganized upon the floor
> She yawns and draws a stocking up;

The poem's second conspirator appears after the waiter brings in exotic fruit:

> Rachel *née* Rabinovitch
> Tears at the grapes with murderous paws;

The remaining characters, if not as active, are just as low.

We know something of Sweeney from Eliot's

other poems. In "Sweeney Erect" we see him shaving naked in a brothel, undisturbed by a girl's shrieking. In "Mr. Eliot's Sunday Morning Service," while others are in church, he shifts from ham to ham in his bath. In the unfinished *Sweeney Agonistes*, he lectures a whore named Doris about life and death, concluding with an anecdote about a man he knew who murdered a girl and kept her corpse in a gallon of lysol in the tub, as the result of which he became something of a philosopher. Critics have differed considerably about the sources of Sweeney, with Eliot's encouragement. Eliot told F. O. Matthiessen that he modelled Sweeney on a man he first saw in a bar in South Boston. He told Nevill Coghill many years later that he pictured Sweeney as a retired professional pugilist who keeps a pub. Conrad Aiken, who knew Eliot well fifty years ago, has written that Sweeney may be modelled on a retired fighter who gave Eliot boxing lessons in South Boston when he was a graduate student in philosophy at Harvard.

Whatever the source of Sweeney, his nature is fairly clear. He is the type of the physical or sensual man. The poem's simple action is a suggestion of conspiracy. We are told of Rachel in the seventh stanza:

> She and the lady in the cape
> Are suspect, thought to be in league;
> Therefore the man with heavy eyes
> Declines the gambit, shows fatigue,

The heavy-eyed man, described merely as "The silent man in mocha brown" or "The silent vertebrate in brown," may be the object of the conspiracy, and appears to think he is, since he departs abruptly in the next stanza, but the larger framework of the poem suggests that it is Sweeney's death that is plotted, and the man in brown may be declining the chance to be a conspirator. There is some possibility that the whole poem after the second stanza is Sweeney's dream, since it is all one enormous sentence introduced by the line:

> And Sweeney guards the hornèd gate.

which might be the Gate of Horn in the *Odyssey* and the *Aeneid* through which true dreams come. Whether the action is dream or real, however, it is distinguished by its sordidity and the subhumanity of the characters: Sweeney is ape, zebra and giraffe, the lap-sitter is "the person in the Spanish cape," Brown is a vertebrate, Rachel tears her food like an animal. Unlike Bianca in Elizabeth Barrett Browning's "Bianca among the Nightingales," Sweeney is a brute among the brutes.

The analogues of the action, however, are considerably less brutish. The last six lines of the poem make it clear that past and present meet in the timeless concurrence of so much of Eliot's poetry, and the singing of the nightingales joins the plot against Sweeney with several famous deeds of violence:

> The nightingales are singing near
> The Convent of the Sacred Heart,

And sang within the bloody wood
When Agamemnon cried aloud,
And let their liquid siftings fall
To stain the stiff dishonoured shroud.

The poem's epigraph is a Greek line from the *Agamemnon* of Aeschylus, Agamemnon's terrible cry as Clytemnestra hacks at him:

Alas, I have been struck deep a deadly wound.

The epigraph and the poem's ending in combination suggest strongly that Sweeney is to be killed, that he is in fact a type of Agamemnon, apeneck and gross, sinful and arrogant in his sin, and that we are at the "purpose" stage of tragedy. The "bloody wood" in which the nightingales sang is, Grover Smith says in *T. S. Eliot's Poetry and Plays*, the grove of the Furies in Sophocles' *Oedipus at Colonus*, but it seems much more strongly Sir James Frazer's golden-bough grove in which the sacrifice of the vegetation spirit in various human embodiments goes on eternally.

In an earlier printing, the poem had for its epigraph, not the line from Aeschylus, but a quotation from the anonymous *Raigne of King Edward the Third:*

Why should I speak of the nightingale? The
nightingale sings of adulterous wrong.

The reference is to the myth of Philomela from Ovid's *Metamorphoses*. Her brother-in-law King

Tereus raped her and cut out her tongue to conceal the crime, and the gods transformed her into a nightingale. Eliot used the story as a motif in *The Waste Land* three years later:

> Above the antique mantel was displayed
> As though a window gave upon the sylvan
>   scene
> The change of Philomel, by the barbarous king
> So rudely forced; yet there the nightingale
> Filled all the desert with inviolable voice
> And still she cried, and still the world pursues,
> "Jug Jug" to dirty ears.

"Sylvan scene," incidentally, is from Book Four of *Paradise Lost*, Satan's entry into Eden, and Eliot thus makes Philomela and Tereus one more telling of the story of Proserpina gathered by gloomy Dis, *Eliot's* equivalent for Satan's victory over Eve. "Sweeney Among the Nightingales" thus ends with mutilated Philomela singing "with inviolable voice" while Agamemnon lies butchered, and the sacrificial victims in the bloody wood Sweeney is entering begin to pile up.

Nor are those all. The great god Dionysus himself, endlessly dismembered by his band of maenads and endlessly resurrected, appears in stanza five with his attribute the grapes. It is he who is torn apart when Rachel tears the grapes with murderous paws, and the purple juice shed is his blood. Her murderous animal madness is the sign of his entering into her, she eats him to become him, and Dionysus is thus a divine mystery, both slayer and slain. We are then told that the man with heavy eyes:

> Leaves the room and reappears
> Outside the window, leaning in,
> Branches of wistaria
> Circumscribe a golden grin;

He is now the resurrected Dionysus, framed in the purple blood of wistaria, grinning and golden like the Stranger in *The Bacchae*. Half hidden behind him is yet another slain god, Jesus. The poem continues:

> The host with someone indistinct
> Converses at the door apart,
> The nightingales are singing near
> The Convent of the Sacred Heart,

The nightingales now are the nuns singing the Sacred Heart of Jesus and his Passion, Jesus like Dionysus the god sacrificed to the god. The "someone indistinct" with whom the host converses is the indistinct additional figure of *The Waste Land*, "wrapt in a brown mantle, hooded," who is the risen Christ at Emmaus. The man in brown, like Philomela, has been considerably transformed. "The host" himself, in a bold pun, is the sacramental wafer of Communion, and "converses" is the "turns-into" of "conversion," another transformation or metamorphosis. The poem, Donald Stauffer says finely in *The Nature of Poetry*, is a "narrative of betrayal by the brute lust of the world." While Sweeney laughs in a South Boston joint, Eve is corrupted by Satan, Persephone is gathered by Hades, Philomela is raped by Tereus, Agamemnon is slain by Clytemnestra, Dionysus is torn apart by maenads and resurrected, Jesus is betrayed by Judas, crucified, and risen.

The poem then has its seriousness, if low rather than high seriousness. Eliot has Milton in mind not only in *The Waste Land's* "sylvan scene," but in the very Miltonic "maculate," in the first stanza of "Sweeney Among the Nightingales," restoring "immaculate" to its Latin root-meaning of *physically* unspotted. The second and third stanzas set the action against the Miltonic epic setting of geography and cosmology:

> The circles of the stormy moon
> Slide westward toward the River Plate,
> Death and the Raven drift above
> And Sweeney guards the hornèd gate.
>
> Gloomy Orion and the Dog
> Are veiled; and hushed the shrunken seas;

The "shrunken seas" may even be Arnold's shrunken seas of Faith in "Dover Beach." The poem's last line, "To stain the stiff dishonoured shroud," is borrowed from a line in "Ichabod," John Greenleaf Whittier's bitter poem against Daniel Webster, "To stain the dim dishonored brow." Betrayal goes on in New England too, if lesser betrayal. The poem's organization is associative, lyric, and thematic, building up its figures in layers of significance. But its action is a firm sequence of strong verbs, most of them monosyllabic: Sweeney spreads, guards; Miss Cape tries, slips, pulls, overturns, yawns, draws; Brown sprawls, withdraws, declines, leaves, reappears; Rachel tears; the nightingales sang and Agamemnon cried.

One of the things the poem is about is art. The title "Sweeney Among the Nightingales," in this aspect, is a conceit for the poet and his low subject. The inviolable voice of Philomela that tells her woes after her tongue has been cut out (in the myth, she weaves her story into a piece of embroidery) is art: embroidery, Ovid's poetry, Aeschylus singing the death of Agamemnon, Eliot singing the conspiracy against Sweeney. At the end of the poem, the liquid siftings of the nightingales that fall on Agamemnon's corpse are the pure notes of immortal song. But they are also bird droppings, spotting the dishonoured shroud, making it maculate instead of immaculate. Another of the things the poem is about is excrement. The lovely song of the nightingale is "'Jug Jug' to dirty ears," and if the sacramental drinking of Dionysus in the grape or eating of Christ in the wafer is high spiritual experience at one end of the process, it is excrement at the other. Eliot's poem is the voice of the modern revolution, insisting against Arnold that poetry must deal with the most sordid details of experience as well as the noblest, and embodying both in Sweeney. Eliot told Matthiessen, in a characteristic statement, "that all he consciously set out to create in 'Sweeney Among the Nightingales' was a sense of foreboding." This may very well be true, but its truth is the cryptic ironic truth of the Delphic oracle. Eliot was not doing an ominous saloon scene, but offering us the deepest forebodings of the human spirit: that man is only a nasty animal; that the dead may not rise; that God's death may be, as Yeats said, "but a play"; that art is merely the child's fouling of his crib.

THE SANCTION for "Sweeney Among the Nightingales" is Eliot's essay "Tradition and the Individual Talent," published the next year, 1919, and collected in a volume, *The Sacred Wood*, in 1920. "Tradition and the Individual Talent" discusses the relationship of a modern poet to his predecessors, the nature of the poetic process, and the aims of poetry and the poet. In it Eliot never mentions "Sweeney Among the Nightingales," nor any of his poems, nor even the fact that he is a poet. The essay is nevertheless a powerful manifesto for his own individual talent. *The Sacred Wood*, Matthiessen writes in *The Achievement of T. S. Eliot*, immediately placed the author "in the main line of poet-critics that runs from Ben Jonson and Dryden through Samuel Johnson, Coleridge, and Arnold," the line of "craftsmen talking of what they knew at first hand." Eliot was performing his friend Ezra Pound's highest function of criticism, formulating the principles his poetry demonstrates. Many years later, in "The Music of Poetry" in 1942, Eliot admitted this. He wrote:

> But I believe that the critical writings of poets, of which in the past there have been some very distinguished examples, owe a great deal of their interest to the fact that the poet, at the back of his mind, if not as his ostensible purpose, is always trying to defend the kind of poetry he is writing, or to formulate the kind that he wants to write.

The key word in "Tradition and the Individual Talent" is "tradition." Eliot begins by saying that it is used mostly as censure or archaeology, that we tend to dwell on differences, to praise a poet for "those aspects of his work in which he least resembles anyone else." Eliot would have us praise a poet as "traditional" and value his resemblances to earlier poetry, but not for simple copying. He writes:

> Tradition is a matter of much wider significance. It cannot be inherited, and if you want it you must obtain it by great labour.

We may be reminded of Arnold's remark in "Milton":

> But excellence is not common and abundant; on the contrary, as the Greek poet long ago

> said, excellence dwells among rocks hardly accessible, and a man must almost wear his heart out before he can reach her.

A man need not necessarily wear his heart out obtaining tradition, but he must at least ignore his immediate predecessors. Eliot writes, again following Arnold:

> Yet if the only form of tradition, of handing down, consisted in following the ways of the immediate generation before us in a blind or timid adherence to its successes, 'tradition' should positively be discouraged.

In a later essay, "Baudelaire in Our Time," this became the doctrine that tradition skips a generation, and that a poet has more in common with his grandfather's literary generation than with his father's.

In "Tradition and the Individual Talent," Eliot explains that the poet's tradition must be selective but that it cannot be whimsical. He writes:

> To proceed to a more intelligible exposition of the relation of the poet to the past: he can neither take the past as a lump, an indiscriminate bolus, nor can he form himself wholly on one or two private admirations, nor can he form himself wholly upon one preferred period.

Eliot adds:

> The poet must be very conscious of the main current, which does not at all flow invariably through the most distinguished reputations.

Obtaining a tradition requires a special ability. Eliot writes:

> It involves, in the first place, the historical sense, which we may call nearly indispensable to anyone who would continue to be a poet beyond his twenty-fifth year; and the historical sense involves a perception, not only of the pastness of the past, but of its presence; the historical sense compels a man to write not merely with his own generation in his bones, but with a feeling that the whole of the literature of Europe from Homer and within it the whole of the literature of his own country has a simultaneous existence and composes a simultaneous order. This historical sense, which is a sense of the timeless as well as of the temporal and of the timeless and of the temporal together, is what makes a writer traditional. And it is at the same time what makes a writer most acutely conscious of his place in time, of his own contemporaneity.

In this mystic timelessness and simultaneity, we can see the sanction for "Sweeney Among the Nightingales," just as the poem in turn helps us to understand what the essay means. Put more dramatically:

> The existing monuments form an ideal order among themselves, which is modified by the introduction of the new (the really new) work of art among them.

When he wrote that the historical sense is a requisite for the poet over twenty-five, Eliot was thirty-one. In the introduction to the book, he quoted Arnold's remark that the Romantic poets of the first quarter of the nineteenth century "did not know enough," and his clear resolve is not to share that fate.

The poets mentioned in "Tradition and the Individual Talent" are a curious small group: Homer, Aeschylus, Dante, Shakespeare, Tourneur, and Keats. It is not meant to be an inclusive list, and other essays in the book make it clear that the Elizabethan and Jacobean dramatists and the French symbolists share Eliot's esteem. The name of Milton is a marked omission. For years, Pound had been fulminating against Milton: Milton "shows a complete ignorance of the things of the spirit"; "Milton is the most unpleasant of English poets"; "Milton is the worst sort of poison," "the worst possible food for a growing poet"; and so on. Eliot did not publish on Milton until 1936, in "A Note on the Verse of John Milton," and then to explain that Milton was an unsatisfactory human being and a bad influence, concluding: "He may still be considered as having done damage to the English language from which it has not wholly recovered." When Eliot ate some of his words in "The Music of Poetry" in 1942 and a second essay on Milton in 1947 (all of these are reprinted in *On Poetry and Poets*), he conceded that he had blamed Milton for too much that was inevitable in the history of culture, and that if Milton made blank verse impossible for the drama, "we may also believe that dramatic blank verse had exhausted its resources, and had no future in any event." The point of all of this is that Milton had no place in 1918 in *Eliot's* poetic tradition, that another kind of poetry had to be written.

Eliot's account of the poetic process in "Tradition and the Individual Talent" centers in the image of the catalyst, "the action which takes place when a bit of finely filiated platinum is introduced into a chamber containing oxygen and sulphur dioxide." Eliot writes:

> When the two gases previously mentioned are mixed in the presence of a filament of platinum, they form sulphurous acid. This combination takes place only if the platinum is present; nevertheless the newly formed acid contains no trace of platinum, and the platinum itself is apparently unaffected; has remained inert, neutral, and unchanged. The mind of the poet is the shred of platinum.

We cannot doubt that the catalyst analogy is aimed at Arnold's touchstones. A touchstone is a flintlike stone used to test the purity of gold and silver. By replacing Arnold's primitive image with an up-to-date scientific one, by transferring the operation from the reading process to the writing process (the poet's mind being platinum, more precious than gold and silver), and by nastily imaging the poem as sulphurous acid, Eliot is producing an ironic counterstatement.

The formal theory that follows from the catalyst analogy, as "high seriousness" followed from the touchstone, is what Eliot calls "this Impersonal theory of poetry." Eliot got it from Pound, who got it ultimately from Poe. "The more perfect the artist," he writes, "the more completely separate in him will be the man who suffers and the mind which creates." Eliot adds: "The poet has, not a 'personality' to express, but a particular medium." Thus:

> Poetry is not a turning loose of emotion, but an escape from emotion; it is not the expression of personality, but an escape from personality. But, of course, only those who have personality and emotions know what it means to want to escape from these things.

He concludes: "The emotion of art is impersonal." In the essay "Hamlet and His Problems" written the same year, Eliot amplified the Impersonal theory with the doctrine, built on Wordsworth's formula, of the "objective correlative":

> a set of objects, a situation, a chain of events which shall be the formula of that *particular* emotion; such that when the external facts, which must terminate in sensory experience, are given, the emotion is immediately evoked.

The ingredients of poetry are the poet's emotions and feelings, with a somewhat shadowy distinction between them, and it will evoke emotions and feelings in the reader, but as the link between those two experiences it is not itself emotional or feeling. In his essay "Dante" in 1929, Eliot repudiates his earlier prejudice "that poetry not only must be found *through* suffering but can find its material only *in* suffering," which found expression in such statements as the one in "Shakespeare and the Stoicism of Seneca":

> Shakespeare, too, was occupied with the struggle—which alone constitutes life for a poet—to transmute his personal and private agonies into something rich and strange, something universal and impersonal.

Emotions and feelings are thus visibly suffering and agonies, but the poem is to be an artifact to produce them without displaying them. Poetry is "a fusion of elements," and a great variety of combinations is possible. The nightingales will sing for Sweeney too.

Finally, the aim of poetry is delight, as it was for earlier critics. Eliot writes:

> if we seek not Blue-book knowledge but the enjoyment of poetry, and ask for a poem, we shall seldom find it.

Eliot goes directly after Arnold's "high seriousness," tagging it as the Longinean criterion it is. He writes:

> If you compare several representative passages of the greatest poetry you see how great is the variety of types of combination, and also how completely any semi-ethical criterion of 'sublimity' misses the mark. For it is not the 'greatness,' the intensity, of the emotions, the components, but the intensity of the artistic process, the pressure, so to speak, under which the fusion takes place, that counts.

Here, finally, is what will allow the "low seriousness" of "Sweeney Among the Nightingales" to be great poetry, the intensity of the fusion. Eliot has attacked Arnold for not being "altogether the detached critic" but having his own poetry in mind when he wrote, and we are reminded of Wyndham Lewis' statement in *Men Without Art* that Eliot always describes himself in accusing Arnold. The last sentence of "Tradition and the Individual Talent" is a manifesto for the new poet:

> And he is not likely to know what is to be done unless he lives in what is not merely the present, but the present moment of the past, unless he is

conscious, not of what is dead, but of what is already living.

In his later account of the poet-critic in "The Music of Poetry," Eliot wrote:

> Especially when he is young, and actively engaged in battling for the kind of poetry which he practises, he sees the poetry of the past in relation to his own: and his gratitude to those dead poets from whom he has learned, as well as his indifference to those whose aims have been alien to his own, may be exaggerated. He is not so much a judge as an advocate. His knowledge even is likely to be partial: for his studies will have led him to concentrate on certain authors to the neglect of others. When he theorizes about poetic creation, he is likely to be generalizing one type of experience; when he ventures into aesthetics, he is likely to be less, rather than more competent than the philosopher; and he may do best merely to report, for the information of the philosopher, the data of his own introspection. What he writes about poetry, in short, must be assessed in relation to the poetry he writes.

It is the man of fifty-four looking back on the man of thirty-one, who found in the tradition of the past, as Eliot wrote in "Yeats," "the kind of poetry that is in him to write." The young Eliot thus created the taste by which he was to be enjoyed, and

"Tradition and the Individual Talent" made it possible for "Sweeney Among the Nightingales," and poems like it before and after, to survive in the world of Milton and the mighty dead without conceding an inch. That is the true relation between poetry and criticism, a marriage based on mutual need, and as marriages go it has been an unusually fruitful and happy one over the centuries.

Stanley Edgar Hyman

is a member of the literature faculty at Bennington College in Bennington, Vermont, and has been a staff writer for *The New Yorker* magazine since his graduation from Syracuse University in 1940. Author of a book of literary criticism, *The Armed Vision,* and the editor of another, *The Critical Performance*, Mr. Hyman was awarded a fellowship in 1959 by the American Council of Learned Societies. A native of New York City, Mr. Hyman now lives in North Bennington with his wife, Shirley Jackson, and their four children.